"And we will continue together until the road vanishes..."

from a poem Che wrote to Aleida.

REMEMBERING CHE

MY LIFE WITH CHE GUEVARA

Aleida March

Centro de Estudios
CHE GUEVARA

NEW YORK • OAKLAND • LONDON

Published in English by Seven Stories Press, Inc., New York, on behalf of Ocean
Press, Melbourne, and the Che Guevara Studies Center, Havana.

Published in Spanish by Seven Stories Press, Inc., New York and Ocean Sur,
Melbourne as Evocación

Library of Congress Cataloging-in-Publication Data

Names: March de la Torre, Aleida, author. | 1 Aguilar, Pilar, transla | 2
    Centro de Estudios Che Guev
Title: 10 Remembering Che : my life with Che Guevara / Aleida March ;
    translated by Pilar Agui
Other titles: Evocación. Eng | 30 My life with Che Gue
Description: English edit | 1 North Melbourne, Victoria, Australia :
    Ocean Press, [2 | Series: 0 The Che Guevara lib | "Published in
    Spanish as "Evocación: Mi vida al lado del Che," ISBN: 97819217001
Identifiers: LCCN 2022053538 | ISBN 9781644212059 (trade paperback) | ISBN
    9781644212066 (ebook)
Subjects: LCSH: 0 Cuba--History--1
Classification: LCC F1788.22.M34 A313 2023 | DDC 972.9106/4092
    [B]--dc23/eng/20221109
LC record available at https://lccn.loc.gov/2022053538

Also published by Seven Stories Press/Ocean Sur in Spanish as
Evocación, ISBN 978-1-64421-207-3 (paperback);
ISBN 978-1-64421-208-0 (ebook)

Printed in the USA

9 8 7 6 5 4 3 2 1

CONTENTS

Publisher's note for the English edition

The publishers of this English edition of *Evocación: Mi vida al lado del Che* by Aleida March would like to thank the following people for their contribution to this book:

Jo Connolly, Christine Graunas, Vanessa Hutchinson, Runa Kamijo, María del Carmen Ariet, Lidoly Chávez, Rachel Kirby and Pilar Aguilera, for her sensitive translation.

Above all, we would like to thank Aleida March herself for being prepared to share for the first time her memories of a great legend and a great love.

OUR ALEIDA

She held her silence for decades, finding refuge on another plane. Aleida March drew strength from her pain and then dedicated her life to planting the seed of irrepressible memory. In this book, she has given us something authentic, profound, complex and rich.

Moreover, her memories are remarkably precise and astute. Oblivion can take different forms: To perpetuate Che as a myth, an ideal, is to assign him to oblivion. As the icon of liturgies is also oblivion for Che, as is Che gazing into the future as seen through the lens of Korda—Korda the poet. Similarly, the left that does not struggle, and is sluggish of mind, can no longer be considered left—it, too, is destined for oblivion.

Memory is sown in a different way—through immortal texts, supported by an immortal example. Action as the result of a material expression of thought can be the inspiration for a new generation, one that knows how to struggle relentlessly, indefatigably, with clarity and courage.

Our Aleida, the revolutionary, despite her doubts, has shown she knows how to give. She knew that pain is nourished by the blood of martyrs and the blood of the universe. In this book she now reveals to us the Che that was missing, the loving Che, with an affection that transcends love. An eternity of love, when the essence of a life lived is revealed. A love that transcends tenderness and has nothing to do with abstract idealism. It is a love that is returned to the person offering it, and in that person finds its dwelling place.

This young urban guerrilla, who was shaped by the struggle, now many years later bravely offers herself to us in letters, notes, poems and reflections on a life full of pain, fulfillment, challenges, transgression and heartbreak. This was the love lived. Here Aleida shows us how a personality grew, how it was discovered and displayed. She shares the meeting that marked forever how two lives became united.

She shows us how these lifetimes can define one's destiny. How the fragile nature of a poet can reside within steel — the "poet" who unleashed hurricanes. I knew that poet who unleashed hurricanes, and I knew that young woman of firm convictions. They knew the secret of love. How fortunate it is that she has been able to share with the reader some of this story, by extracting memories from her well-guarded intimacy as a way of sharing her beloved and thereby allowing us to come to know him better.

For all of that, Aleida, many thanks.

Alfredo Guevara
Havana

DEDICATION

To my children,
My greatest source of inspiration.

To Fidel,
To whom I owe everything.

To Alfredo Guevara,
A friend for all times.

To Abel Prieto and Roberto Fernández Retamar,
Patrons of a different kind and of a new era.

To María del Carmen Ariet,
A friend, always willing to offer her help.

To Camilo Pérez,
Thank you for your much appreciated support.

PREFACE

One afternoon I held a tape recorder in my hands to collect my memories. But although I tried, I found I just couldn't do it. So I discussed this with my friend and collaborator, María del Carmen Ariet.

At the time, I was working to create the Che Guevara Studies Center. Together, María del Carmen and I had archived Che's documents, photographs, letters, poems and other personal items. It was a huge challenge. From that project emerged the plan to publish systematically all Che's works. We wanted new generations to be able to know Che and understand what he fought for, to help young people feel close to him, not just as a symbol but as a real person who, from an early age, had great dreams and realized those dreams with a creative spirit.

As the Che Guevara Studies Center has developed, we have not only aspired to encourage the study of Che's thought, life and example, but also to work with our local community in Havana to promote one of his most important qualities — ethics — so that they can understand the better world he fought for.

A few years ago, Mr. Giuseppe Cecconi, a gentle and persistent Italian man, approached me; he wanted me to write a script for a film he was making about Che. I wasn't particularly interested in that project, but I realized that, apart from anything else, I owed it to my children to give my account of my life with Che. So I began to write down my recollections, everything I had lived through, everything we had experienced together.

This book is therefore my recollections, nothing more. I am not a writer. I simply put down on paper my most cherished memories, hoping that readers might appreciate what it cost me to share these precious letters and poems that until now I held so close to my heart.

Aleida March

Time, time that always passes.
It might be oblivion to forget,
a memory blown away like ash,
ash left to settle that can easily disperse,
disperse with the slightest breeze.
That is life, or tends to be life.
We must understand it and confront it.
I exist, nevertheless. I act and I even write,
and I am filled with love.

Alfredo Guevara

1

When I was very young, I loved to read romantic literature. Among the books I read was the novel *Headless Angel* by the Austrian author Vicki Baum and it awoke in me an urge to know more about the history of Latin America. My thirst for this knowledge led me to ask my friends for books about the Mexican revolution. This might seem insignificant now, but with the passing of time memories of one's youth seem to become more vivid. I think in a way my life parallels that of the protagonist of the story in that book.

I have never fancied myself as a writer, probably because when it comes to writing my standards have always been set high, and I feel I can't meet that standard. Nevertheless, I have written what could be considered the brief story of my life. Writing about my own life also provided an opportunity to narrate some of my memories of Che.

In this short account, I don't want to highlight some moments over others. If I were to do so, I might run the risk of making mistakes or letting myself be swayed by subjective factors, and this would divert me from my original purpose.

It is quite a daunting task to describe my personal experiences with a man who, well before he was my partner, was already recognized as a remarkable individual. Of course my perspective is colored by our shared experiences and our shared political commitment. I made that commitment willingly and, as I have stressed, in many ways I had to abandon my individuality to become less of an "I" and more of a "we." I have never regretted this.

The story begins with my first encounter with Commander Ernesto Che Guevara in the Escambray Mountains during the revolutionary war in Cuba. My first contact with the guerrillas occurred when Che and his column moved west, down from the Sierra Maestra in the former province of Oriente, into central Cuba. Che, an Argentine, with an already well-deserved reputation, was the leader of the Eighth Column. I was active in the urban underground movement and was sent on a mission by local leaders of the July 26 Movement. Our province (formerly known as Las Villas) was surrounded and closely monitored by repressive forces of the Batista dictatorship.* My mission was to act as a courier, delivering money and documents to the rebels when they reached the Escambray Mountains.

It was a dangerous mission and this was my first chance to have direct contact with the guerrilla movement. On reaching the rebels' camp, I found they were observing me as much as I observed them. Some of the guerrillas couldn't figure me out at all, wondering what on earth I was doing there. This wasn't particularly surprising because I hardly looked like a tough guerrilla fighter. I was quite a pretty young woman, looking anything but a battle-ready combatant.

My famous "first encounter" with Che has been somewhat

---

* Fulgencio Batista y Zalivar (1901-1973) participated in the military coup that took place September 4, 1933.. The conservatives used him as a US stooge in the overthrow of the Grau-Guiteras government in 1934. He then ruled Cuba until 1944. On March 10, 1952, he organized another coup and initiated a bloody dictatorship. He fled Cuba along with a group of cronies in the early hours of January 1, 1959.

embellished by many writers and journalists. In reality, it had nothing to do with fairy tales and Prince Charmings. Even though the Escambray Mountains are incredibly beautiful and the ideal setting for enchantment, those of us there at that time weren't able to focus on the surrounding natural beauty.

Some years had to pass before I learned what Che had thought of our first encounter. In a letter he sent from the Congo in 1965, a letter full of nostalgia, he revealed what he had thought when he saw me the first time and in the days that followed. He described how he felt torn between his role as a strictly disciplined revolutionary and as an ordinary man with emotional and other needs. He remembered me as a "little blonde, slightly chubby teacher." When he saw the marks left by the adhesive tape around my waist,* he "felt an internal struggle between the (almost) irreproachable revolutionary and the other — the real one — overcome by shyness, while pretending to be the untouchable revolutionary."

It was some time before we were able to acknowledge and then express our feelings for each other. Before doing that, we had to endure some terrifying moments and a few misunderstandings…

---

* Aleida had brought a package containing money to the guerrilla camp in a pouch strapped around her waist with adhesive tape.

2

From the moment of that initial meeting, without my even realizing it, my life took a certain turn and I never looked back. I became involved in crucial events, now part of our country's history. The memories come back to me like flashes of lightning. The intensity of events left no time for lengthy reflection. I felt we were living at a unique time, but we had no idea what the future might bring. Surprisingly, I came closer to really knowing myself, not because I feared death, because we were always aware of it, but rather because I was always challenging myself about what had led me there and about how strong my commitment really was.

Before I found myself in the guerrilla camp in the Escambray, my life had been like that of most other *campesinos*.* Poverty, humiliation and violence were bitter realities in our lives.

I lived in Los Azules, so called, according to my mother, because of the color of the water in the river in earlier times. This was some distance from Santa Clara, the capital city of the former province of Las Villas, in the center of Cuba. It was an idyllic place with beautiful scenery. My world was the small piece of land that my father worked with much determination and, which despite his great efforts, was never very productive. I sometimes agreed with my mother, who saw it as the end of the world. We were

---

* The use of the term *campesinos* includes small farmers, tenant farmers (or peasants) and rural workers.

surrounded by uncles and aunts and other poor neighbors, who had no hope for a better future.

I remember how the little kids would have fun swimming in the river while the older children would have chores to do. I was the youngest of five siblings: Lidia, Estela, Octavio, Orlando and me. I was completely unplanned by my parents and when I came into the world my older sisters were already interested in boys and dating. Lidia was 16 years old and my unexpected arrival was a cause for embarrassment, especially in those prudish times. The reason for the embarrassment was the fertility of my older parents, but I had a happy childhood within the small world of my family. My parents were strong and energetic, poor tenant farmers. But despite the difficulties they faced and their unfavorable situation, they did everything possible to encourage and improve the lives of their offspring.

My father, Juan March, was of Catalan origin, a typical *campesino*, but one who hailed from the city, which gave him a particular air. He liked to read and was cultured to some degree. He was honorable and egalitarian, but also quite introverted. My mother, Eudoxia de la Torre, was the complete opposite. She was a pure *campesina* with a fierce character, stubborn and persistent, who made sure we got by with what we had. They built a home founded on firm moral principles. They met all our basic needs with love, not by spoiling us or with excessive displays of affection, something not the norm among *campesinos*, who live very hard lives. We felt the love and support of our parents and we felt secure in the sense they would do everything they could for us.

My family experienced tragedies. Before I was born, my brother Osvaldo had died, leaving both my parents with a grief they never really overcame. My brother always remained present in our home. It was the custom to pay homage to departed loved ones by keeping photographs of them in the main room. In our home, the treasured photos were of my brother and my paternal grandparents.

Death was, however, a daily occurrence in the countryside, the result of the government's corruption, neglect and apathy toward those living in the country. The rural poor often died because of a lack of medical care, often without ever knowing the exact cause of death. There were no roads or public transport in rural areas, and this meant a lack of access. Often the sick person could not be reached in time.

I was an innocent country girl, happy with my life. I was like a little bird, with few restrictions on my freedom in a beautiful landscape, surrounded by the beauty of nature. Behind my mother's back I would go off riding horses and, while my sisters and mother washed clothes in the river, I would enjoy myself swimming with my cousins. We used the palm tree fronds to make skis to slide down the slopes into the river. There was nothing like it!

I still see myself as that peasant girl, a mixture of my parents with the strong influence of my father, a timid, quiet, not very expressive man. But I'm also restless and like to dream, a tendency that drew me closer to my mother, whose strength and spirit I always admired. I have to admit I cry easily, even to this day, probably due to being the youngest child of the family. Maybe I was a bit spoilt.

If I had to mention anyone else who helped shape me it would be María Urquijo, my teacher in the little rural school with multiple grades. By the grace and good deeds of my parents, the teacher used to stay at our house during the week. This made me respect and love the school even more, despite the poverty that was evident within its humble walls. Our little school was made strong through the discipline of a teacher who had found her true vocation. She forgot her personal problems — she was poorly paid and had a sick daughter — but she opened the doors of knowledge, despite obvious limitations, giving us a basic education to ensure we weren't ignorant or indolent.

When María was unable to attend classes, Ursula Brito or Gilda Balledor would replace her — both also excellent teachers and wonderful human beings.

Of course, I can't describe my childhood without confessing to some incidents of mischief. I will never forget the day an inspector came to our school, looking very elegant on his horse. I innocently invited him to stay at our house. Looking surprised, he said he could not stay because he would have nowhere to sleep. Without thinking, I told him he could sleep in the same bed as the teacher. You can imagine the look on everyone's face, especially the look on Gilda Balledor's face — she was the substitute teacher who was staying at our house, and she was single.

I developed a great admiration for anyone who knew more than me. I became a diligent student and, even though I was quite reserved, I had a great interest in mathematics, poetry and literature. I developed a curiosity to learn about other worlds and continually set myself new challenges. Even though we had few resources at our disposal, the teachers instilled in us a great sense of patriotism and ethics. On weekends we enjoyed public events honoring José Martí and the patriots in our wars of independence. In this way I developed a love of learning, nature and school, along with the ethical principles encouraged in my home, all elements that have influenced my personality and behavior.

Quite unexpectedly, my mother announced that I was to be sent to live in the town to continue my studies. I confess this was probably the first big challenge of my life. Up to that point, I had lived a life of freedom, in what I thought was the best possible world. I was quite shaken by the sudden possibility of having to leave home. I tried to change my parents' minds; I succeeded in convincing my father, but my mother's will was stronger.

The family had already dispersed to some extent by that time. My older siblings Lidia and Estela had their own homes. Both lived in the town of Santa Clara, which is why my parents were able to send me and my brother Orlando (six years older than me) to study there. So off we went to Santa Clara to live with our sisters and study in town.

Living away from home made me realize how much I needed my parents. I was so happy when my mother came for a visit. Santa Clara was a strange place for me. Although it was very much a provincial town, it expanded my limited horizons. I lived with my older sister, who had a different way of doing things. She worked, so I had to help out with the chores and look after her three children. I felt like a housewife, for which I had little vocation, and at the same time I had to keep up with my studies.

The biggest change for me was at school. I was used to my teacher María and her method of teaching. I was not yet aware of the limitations of my knowledge. I found it difficult to adjust to having homework, with which I struggled, especially English, a language strange and foreign to me. I just couldn't relate to it and I must admit that I still find English hard. Nevertheless, eventually I became acclimatized to my new situation. Because I was young, I soon learned to appreciate the advantages of life in town.

I began upper primary school quite confused. Besides English, we learned music. I had no idea music could be a subject one studied at school. Eventually I was able to adjust with the help of some wonderful, supportive teachers, who introduced me to all kinds of new things.

Often school could be a place of prejudice and other barriers. There was discrimination based on gender, and the school had a militaristic atmosphere and authoritarian approach to discipline.

For example, they would close the windows to stop the girls making contact with the boys. That is how schools were in those days.

Over time I became keenly aware of my limited education. I wasn't used to going to the library, and I didn't know how to search for new information that would help fill the gaps in my knowledge. Sometimes the teachers would ask me to write essays about historical figures I was supposed to know something about, but often I had never heard of them. I remember one such person was the Argentine writer, President Domingo Faustino Sarmiento.

Then an event occurred that made me realize how tentative life can be. My sister Lidia, who had taken me in, suddenly became very ill and died within a short period of time. My parents decided to move to Santa Clara, which meant our family was reunited and we had our first home in town. My mother took charge of Lidia's children—her grandchildren—and my brother Orlando also came to live with us. My mother put aside her pain at the loss of her daughter, and through determination and hard work convinced my father to establish a new home. Our financial difficulties, however, did not end there, but we dealt with them more effectively.

Feeling the love and closeness of my parents helped me focus on my studies with greater enthusiasm. In my new role as "big sister" to my nieces and nephew, I would attend their school meetings. I helped them with their homework until, against our wishes, the boy went to live with his father, who had remarried. One of the twins went to live with my grandmother, and so we were left with only one of the girls.

Once I finished high school, I decided to study education, not because it was the easier option—I wanted to study medicine— but because of money. My family simply lacked the financial resources. Education was a quicker career that could be completed in four years and you could also start working immediately after you graduated — at least that is what I thought at the time.

I sat the very demanding entrance exam. Unfortunately, the gaps in my knowledge were very evident. The best result I got was in mathematics, but my bad grammar meant I failed Spanish. So again supported by my teacher María, I returned to study at a preparatory school in Santa Clara, in order to sit the exams a second time.

While I prepared for my exams I enrolled in the Institute of Secondary Education without taking into account the financial difficulties I might have. I needed books, which I had to buy, and once I finished I would still not be a qualified professional. But I was young and full of hope. I studied without allowing myself to think of failure, aware that if I failed, everything would fall apart. I also played volleyball and softball. I was pitcher of the softball team and I wasn't too bad, drawing on my experience growing up in the countryside. I gave up sports when I became ill and my mother insisted I stop.

I finally passed my exams and began my teacher training at 15; I finished that course successfully in 1953. My brother Orlando supported me and I am very grateful to him for that. One of my uncles paid for my graduation. I was satisfied to have finished my studies and in time I grew to love my career as a teacher. In that same year I went to study pedagogy at the Central University of Las Villas, and this proved to be a very important decision.

Until 1956 my life was centered on study, sport being my only form of recreation, along with reading novels (especially romantic ones), going to the cinema whenever I could and to the park, which in a small town is a type of outing. There were a few young men who courted me, but I never felt in love, although sometimes I made a fool of myself by pretending to be in love. Having romantic dreams about imaginary princes was typical behavior for a young woman living in the provinces, especially one of my social class.

Fulgencio Batista's coup d'etat in March 1952 was the first political event to have an impact on me. My parents favored neither political side, although my father, like the majority of Cuban people at the time, had placed his hopes in the Authentics,* particularly in the man who came after the fraudulent government of Ramón Grau San Martín. Later, he supported the Cuban Revolutionary Party (Orthodox) under the leadership of Eduardo Chibás. Its slogan was, "Honor against money."**

I remember everyone's shock on March 10 when General Batista seized power. Everyone expected another corrupt regime, one even more subservient to the United States. When I left school that day, I went to the Institute of Secondary Education, near my home, to see what was happening. I expected it to be the center of protests against Batista. But everything there was quiet.

The following year, 1953, was the year of my political awakening. I heard stories about the July 26 attack led by Fidel Castro on the Moncada military barracks in Santiago de Cuba and its tragic aftermath when so many young people were rounded up and

---

* The Cuban Revolutionary Party (Authentic) was formed after the failed revolution of 1933, when revolutionary elements united to win the election. The party held power between 1944 and 1948, under Ramón Grau San Martín, the party's main figurehead. He did not fulfill his electoral promises and was succeeded by Carlos Prío Socarrás in 1948. His government was characterized by corruption and inefficiency, which eroded support for the Authentics. Fulgencio Batista took advantage of the political discontent and organized a coup on March 10, 1952.

** The Orthodox Party was formed in reaction to corruption of the Cuban Revolutionary Party (Authentic). The left wing of the Authentic party split away and called themselves "authentic-orthodox." Led by Eduardo Chibás, in 1947 they opposed President Grau, and formed a new party, the Cuban Revolutionary Party (Orthodox), based primarily on the *creole* (national) bourgeoisie. The majority of the Cuban people supported this new party. Their slogan, "Honor against money," struck a chord with the nation. Fidel Castro became a member of this party's radical wing.

murdered in cold blood. The name of Fidel Castro now became familiar to some Cubans, who learned about his role in the student movement at the University of Havana and his affiliation to the Orthodox Party.

Most people, however, remained cynical after decades of politicking and empty promises. When I found out what had happened in Santiago de Cuba I became curious to know more about this Fidel Castro, the man who was reviving the ideas of our 19th century national hero José Martí with clarity and political vision.

After the joy of my graduation had subsided, I also learned pretty quickly about government corruption. It was impossible to gain a teaching position without handing over a large bribe. And even then, the post would be in some tiny school with multiple grades in a remote area.

My political education really began during my time at university. As I wasn't yet a fully qualified teacher, I enrolled in the pedagogy faculty at the Central University of Las Villas. The university was reopening after a period of closure following Batista's coup, and was trying to establish itself as one of the few elite universities that existed in Cuba in those days. The others were the University of Havana and the recently founded University of Oriente in Santiago de Cuba. This was a noble effort by the professors of the Central University, who tried to set the same educational standards as their counterparts at other institutions.

I took advantage of the free enrolment offered to students with good grades. I overcame the weaknesses of my academic development and tried to broaden my horizons, exploring all kinds of new things. I studied subjects like psychology, which I found most stimulating, and I spent more time reading serious books, although I did still enjoy reading romantic novels.

At university I formed close friendships, some through the Presbyterian Church. I had adopted that faith before going to university, because it was closer to my world and seemed very different from the Catholic religion. I thought the Catholic Church was full of pomp and hypocrisy, representing only the rich and powerful.

The Presbyterian Church seemed to allow more freedom of thought and was more in keeping with the times. Its members, ideas and interests were closer to mine. I still have friends from that time such as Sergio Arce and Orestes González, who are Presbyterian pastors and who have always been kind and understanding.

My studies remained the main focus of my attention for another three years. I was always walking a financial tightrope because I had not come from a well-off family. I kept searching for a teaching position, but jobs were scarce or nonexistent for women not prepared to offer up their bodies or honor in exchange for employment. The most one could aspire to was a poorly paid job in a private school or teaching private classes.

Meanwhile the political climate heated up and discontent spread among the population, at the same time as the repression increased. There were rumors that Fidel Castro, who had been convicted and imprisoned, had been granted an amnesty and freed from prison on the Isle of Pines. We heard that the July 26 Movement had been formed to honor the date of the audacious attack on the Moncada barracks. There was talk that Fidel had gone into exile in Mexico and that he made speeches there, promising to return to Cuba to liberate the country.

1956 was a decisive year for me. I carefully studied an underground copy of *History will Absolve Me*, Fidel's defense speech at his trial for the Moncada attack. I was excited to read a document I felt expressed my ideas about how Cuba could attain its dignity as a nation.

The atmosphere at university became tense; the situation deteriorated to the point where, like other universities, it was closed again the following year. This unrest was reflected throughout the nation. Even though the Central University of Las Villas did not have the same radical tradition as the University of Havana, our students opposed the dictatorship and began to organize in response to the continued repression.

By that time, I had completed three of my four years of the pedagogy course, but we were unable to complete our courses after the university closed.

One September afternoon in 1956, I met Faustino Pérez outside my house. He was a fellow Presbyterian, a good, kind man, who inspired such confidence in me that despite my usual timidity, without explaining myself very well, I asked him if I could join the July 26 Movement. Faustino had just come back from Mexico and he eagerly accepted my offer. That was how simple things were back then. I knew Faustino through my Presbyterian friends, Esther and Gladys González. Esther had been my classmate at teacher's college, and Gladys and I became friends at university. We studied together and they shared their books with me; I was always welcomed warmly at their home and felt the affection of their family.

Everything came together around me. Margot Machado, head of the school where I worked in the morning, was an active militant of the July 26 Movement and later we carried out a number of assignments together as clandestine combatants of the movement.

That was the way I became involved in the struggle. Another world then opened to me, and I have always regarded that as the real moment of my birth. From that point, I gave myself to the movement with complete dedication and sacrifice. This was probably one of the happiest times in my life.

3

Why did I describe myself as a "combatant"? That word summed up our commitment to changing the status quo. We had complete confidence and faith in Fidel and were willing to fight in order to end once and for all the shame and moral degradation that Cubans had suffered.

There was no doubt or fear in my mind when, one day not long afterwards, on Faustino's instructions, I approached the pharmacy on the San Pedro bridge. I was going to see Santiago Riera, who was the coordinator of the movement in the province at that time, to tell him I had joined. This was before the arrival of the *Granma* on December 2, 1956, bringing Fidel back from exile in Mexico, along with his intrepid followers.*

Although there wasn't much information about how or when the guerrilla expedition would arrive, the leaders of the July 26 Movement in the province took some measures to support the action, while Santiago Riera returned to Santiago de Cuba to meet with Frank País to find out what was happening. Our group of women, led by Margot Machado, prepared to help by providing first aid to the combatants if there was a clash or wherever else we were needed for other tasks.

We waited anxiously. We heard the initial reports about the

---

* After his release from prison in May 1955, Fidel Castro went into exile in Mexico, where he continued to organize the revolutionary July 26 Movement.

events in Santiago de Cuba. On November 30,* in that town on the east coast of the island, young people led by Frank País initiated actions to support the arrival of the *Granma* and to distract the troops of the Batista dictatorship. Our leading compañeros, Santiago Riera and Guillermo Rodríguez, who had been a part of the National Revolutionary Movement along with Armando Hart and Professor Rafael García Bárcena, arrived to coordinate the actions of our group in Santa Clara. But they only got as far as Camagüey and had to return. We could not contact them and didn't know what to do. In the end nothing happened in Santa Clara. There were no precise instructions for how we could support the landing of the *Granma*, even though Haydee Leal had received instructions from Mexico. The movement had a national structure, but was far from being cohesive. We lacked — and here I include myself — the necessary political education and experience to meet the challenges required by the struggle.

In those early days, Haydee Leal's house was the central meeting place for compañeros of the July 26 Movement leadership in our province. We had the support of her mother, Luisa Díaz. It is important to emphasize it wasn't only young people willing to lend their support to the struggle, but also many mothers, who understood that they, too, had to take a stand and join the movement.

Then we heard alarming news reports about what had happened on December 2 when the *Granma* landed. We were keenly aware of the lies spread on the radio and in the press on

---

* On November 25, 1956, a group of 82 guerrillas left the Mexican port of Tuxpan in a yacht called the *Granma*. In order to distract Batista's forces, Frank País, head of the underground July 26 Movement in the former province of Oriente, organized a general uprising on November 30, the date the expeditionaries were expected to arrive. The plan involved attacks on the headquarters of the National and Maritime Police in Santiago de Cuba in order to obtain arms for the guerrillas and prevent the concentration of the dictatorship's forces. Unfortunately, this was not successful. Moreover, the landing of the *Granma* was delayed until December 2.

behalf of the regime. But because we lacked any real information, we were upset by reports that Fidel had apparently been killed. We were distraught with frustration and bitterness until Faustino came to Santa Clara on one of his short visits, and he confirmed the leader of our movement was alive, fighting in the mountains. He described the landing of the *Granma* at Las Coloradas beach and the clash that had taken place at Alegría de Pío, resulting in the dispersal of the guerrillas.*

I didn't know that I, too, would soon experience my own baptism of fire. I still remember the trepidation I felt when asked to go and meet someone at the home of (Lolita) Dolores Rosell, a friend and fellow combatant. To my surprise, Gino Done, an expeditionary from the *Granma*, who had managed to escape the enemy, had come to Santa Clara to participate in sabotage actions—at least that was what I was told. Gino, an Italian who had fought in the Second World War, was a sailor who had made many trips to Cuba. He had worked as a builder in Havana and elsewhere in Cuba, so he had easily found his way to Santa Clara. The mission Gino had come to complete before January 15, 1957, with me as his accomplice was—believe it or not—to throw a grenade at a Christmas tree that decorated the lobby of the building of the provincial government. The objective of this action was to draw attention to the fact that the insurrection had extended to the center of the island.

Small groups had already been formed to carry out courageous actions and sabotage. One of their first aims was to cut the power lines in order to support the grenade attack on the government building, located in the center of Santa Clara. When I think now about how we prepared for this action, I'm embarrassed, although at the time I felt proud that I had been chosen to carry out such

---

* On December 5, 1956, with the help of *campesinos* from the area, the rebel forces reunited under the leadership of Fidel Castro in the area of Cinco Palmas.

a risky mission. I had to go by Lolita's house that afternoon to pick up the grenade and carry it in one of her handbags. While I waited, I went back home and placed the handbag on top of my wardrobe. I had no idea how to use a grenade and I was totally irresponsible by putting my family at risk, given that anything could have happened.

It was a popular pastime to take a stroll in Vidal Park in the center of town, so nobody at home objected to my going there. I met up again with Gino and, armed with the grenade in the handbag I carried under my arm, we headed toward the government building at the precise time the electricity would be cut off. Just as we were about to execute "the plan," the lights came back on and we had to leave without being able to do anything. All we could do was go back to Lolita's house, return the grenade and go home feeling sad and frustrated. Without overstating it, this was my little Alegría de Pío.

On December 5, 1956, at Alegría de Pío, in the former province of Oriente, Fidel and the other expeditionaries from the *Granma* (including Che, who had joined as the troop's doctor) were caught by surprise by Batista's troops. This episode is vividly narrated by Che in his book *Reminiscences of the Cuban Revolutionary War*. He describes how, after walking for long hours through saltwater swamps, suffering many calamities, the survivors of the *Granma* expedition were completely exhausted. Many of them had lost part of their equipment when they found themselves in an unequal fight in which Che himself was injured. This was the first armed clash for what would become the Rebel Army, and Che described it as their "baptism of fire," even though it did not end in victory.*

We were not entirely aware the tasks we were given would

---

* See "Alegría del Pío" in Ernesto Che Guevara: *Reminiscences of the Cuban Revolutionary War* (Seven Stories Press, 2025).

often endanger the lives of our families. Now I look back and recall the number of times I had to lie in order to leave the house. My parents didn't understand and they certainly couldn't accept that a young woman would put herself and her reputation at risk, especially in the early days when they were not quite sure what I was doing. Sometimes compañeros would risk coming to my house to leave urgent messages for me. My little niece Miriam was always curious when she learned about such visits. Even when my mother told her not to say anything, she would come to me quietly and whisper, "They came to see you."

I would always leave the house with the excuse I was going to study at my friends' home (the González family) or that I was going to work. At the time, my parents never imagined the dangers we faced, or how my activities endangered them also. Batista's repressive forces had no scruples in applying the cruelest forms of torture. Unfortunately we Cubans were among the first to experience some of bloody practices that in later years became widespread throughout Latin America. It is therefore understandable that, when my parents found out what I was doing, they forbade my outings. Although I was young, I was old enough to make my own decisions. I didn't want to hurt anyone and was always clear about my role and what I would and wouldn't do. I know that my parents supported me as best they could, especially towards the end. In fact, my mother accompanied me on more than one occasion, when it was late or when she suspected there might be real danger. As time went by they became more reconciled to my activities and I didn't have to explain myself quite so much, which meant I didn't have to lie. Then one day I didn't return home...

We were always trying to perfect what we did. I had to carry out numerous assignments. There were only a few women and we were very good at distracting enemy soldiers, who became more cruel and despotic as time went on. Under Margot Machado's orders, I often went to key parts of the city alone or sometimes with her. I also worked with Allán Rosell, who was the provincial coordinator of the movement, and with Osvaldo Rodríguez, head of action and sabotage. In 1957 they were the main local leaders of the movement. That year I also worked with Julio Camacho Aguilera and Raúl Peroso, a very special person, who told me about Vilma Espín, Frank País and the other leading compañeros in Santiago de Cuba.

I came to know the municipal leaders of the movement and later the five regional heads at the time. Undoubtedly, because of the knowledge I had gained and the security of certain contacts, I was used more and more frequently. I had knowledge of and participated in the preparations and plans of the provincial leadership. I also knew about the work of most of the other fronts, such as the workers' sector led by David Salvador. I received an order to take him to the house of Guillermito Rodríguez's mother-in-law to stay the night. From there we were to go to Cienfuegos where he would make contact with members of the July 26 Movement and the Revolutionary Directorate.*

On these assignments, I also regularly visited the municipalities of Cienfuegos, Sagua, Placetas and Sancti Spiritus; I passed through Cabaiguán and sometimes I had to go to Cruces and Remedios and end up in Yaguajay. My role was to reinforce the work of the various fronts and sectors, assisting in the work of the propaganda team.

In general, the underground movement was active throughout the entire province of central Cuba, which led to us considering actions on a broader scale. We prepared for an uprising on September 5, 1957, in Cienfuegos.

---

* The Revolutionary Directorate (DRE) was one of the revolutionary movements opposed to Batista. It had been founded by student leader José Antonio Echevarría in 1955.

In the middle of all this activity, in May 1957, one of Margot Machado's children was killed. Her son, Julio Pino Machado, died alongside one of his compañeros, Chiqui Gómez Lubián. It was a terrible, tragic accident, which happened when they were handling an explosive. It meant the loss of two young and valuable lives. I learned of their deaths when I returned from a mission to Sagua. I went to the funeral home immediately. Margot moved us all by delivering words of farewell to her son with extraordinary strength and dignity.

Despite this tragic event we continued to prepare for the September offensive. Margot sent me to Cienfuegos to get an M-1 rifle, but something alerted to me to danger. When I reached Cruces on a bus called *La Ranchuelera,* I stopped off at María's house. She was a spiritualist and was used as the pretext for my trip. I was terrified at the prospect of torture that we knew was relentless and cruel; my greatest fear was pentothal, the "truth drug" that supposedly made a prisoner divulge whatever information their captors wanted. This spelled disaster for many lives and projects and the moral destruction of the individual combatant.

I arrived in Cruces on a Sunday morning. I took all the necessary precautions with my visit to the spiritualist, and then I went to see Enriquito Cañer, chief of action and sabotage in the area. He lived in a nearby sugar-growing town, and he decided to travel with me to Cienfuegos to get the rifle and drive me in his car back to Santa Clara. We returned and headed to Lolita's house where Allán Rosell (coordinator of the July 26 Movement in Las Villas), Emilio Aragonés, Osvaldo Rodríguez and other compañeros were staying. We handed over the weapon without taking many precautions. Margot was horrified at our rashness. We called it a happy irresponsible act because we had completed our mission. In later years when Margot recalled aspects of the struggle, she remembered that incident. Considering the level of danger we had been in, she regretted having sent me on that mission. Nevertheless, I think she was just doing her job. We were all combatants in an underground struggle and there could be no differentiation between us. I believe that this high level of dedication and courage distinguished the combatants in our town from others.

The groundwork for the September 5 uprising was laid in three phases of organization throughout the province. During that period, 35 compañeros of the July 26 Movement were imprisoned due to a betrayal. They had been in a house in Cienfuegos waiting for orders. Despite being savagely tortured, none of them gave away the plans for the offensive and so our preparations continued. The insurrection of September 5, however, did not achieve its desired objectives due to poor organization and logistics. What really limited the possibility of further actions in Cienfuegos was the installation there of a military garrison.

Our combatants displayed great audacity and courage in challenging an enemy that vastly outnumbered them in terms of weaponry. The rebels only retreated when it meant further resistance would be heroic or suicidal. Then we would start over again, never allowing ourselves to be disheartened.

The national leadership of the movement decided to reinforce the province. Julio Camacho Aguilera was the coordinator of the region and his role, in particular, was to organize the September 5 offensive. He left after the uprising failed. Octavio Luis Cabrera was assigned as labor leader and Raúl Peroso became head of action and sabotage. Many of the compañeros, who had been in the leadership, went into hiding in other provinces or were taken prisoner. This caused much instability and was one of the many problems we had to face in our province.

We received an order from Faustino in Havana to contact

Lazaro Artola, who had taken a group of about 40 armed men to the Escambray Mountains. I accompanied Guillermito Rodríguez on a trip there to determine if the conditions were favorable for an uprising in that region. Faustino and other compañeros decided to oppose this initiative, an error that caused more than one problem. There was much misunderstanding by members of the movement about other groups willing to participate in the uprising to extend the guerrilla war to an area offering favorable conditions. This area was later used by rebel forces to great advantage. It was a logical step to open a guerrilla front in the central zone, because it was difficult for many to join the war in the Sierra Maestra. Moreover, it would prove to be a crucial factor in bringing down the dictatorship.

Many of the conflicts between the different groups were due, in part, to the lack of unity in our movement. We did not have a single national unified leadership until after the strike of April 9, 1958. Nevertheless, despite these problems, I felt extraordinarily happy to be participating in such momentous events. I was also proud of the role women were playing in the struggle. I learned of the brutal assassinations of Lidia Doce and Clodomira Acosta, both loyal combatants and valiant messengers for Fidel and Che in the Sierra Maestra. Their example made a huge impression on me.

Some time later, Che told me he had written a piece about them and this was published in the first months of the revolution. He partly based his story about those two heroic women (Lydia and Clodomira) on what I had told him about my own experiences in the underground struggle. Lidia had worked under Che's command in the Sierra Maestra and was devoted to him. Together with Clodomira, she undertook extremely dangerous missions. They were betrayed and brutally murdered. In Che's tribute to these women, published in *Reminiscences of the Cuban Revolutionary War*, he wrote: "I offer these words of remembrance in homage to her today, like a modest flower laid on the vast graveyard this once joyful island became."*

I was rather upset when I learned from Margot Machado that Haydee Santamaría** had been at her house and I had not had the chance to meet her, probably because they took extra precautions for her safety. After the revolution, I had the chance to tell Haydee how disappointed I was not to have met her on that occasion as she had always been a great inspiration to us. She was a woman I really admired, and she continued to amaze me with her courage and fine sensibility in later years.

Many important actions took place throughout the island at the start of 1958. Some of these were organized by the national leadership of the movement and others were initiated by local leaders, who were backed up by the rebel troops. These actions shook the foundations of the dictatorship. During the month of February we got a new coordinator, Enrique Oltuski, whom I introduced to the leaders. We began the formation of July 26 Movement guerrilla fronts, based on Víctor Bordón's earlier initiative at Quemado de Güines. I later met Víctor Bordón in person.

I participated in the creation of almost all of these guerrilla fronts. My role was a practical one, determining their needs for weapons, clothes and whatever else we had at our disposal. I remember visiting Mongo (Faustino) Pérez sometime just before or after the April 9 strike in Santiago and also Julio Chaviano in Santo Domingo or La Esperanza. I had known Chaviano and his family for some time. In this way, we coordinated our work

---

* See Ernesto Che Guevara: *Reminiscences of the Cuban Revolutionary War* (Seven Stories Press, 2025).

** Haydee Santamaría was one of the two women who participated in the July 26, 1953, armed attack on the Moncada barracks in Santiago de Cuba. She was captured and imprisoned. During the revolutionary war, she fought as a guerrilla in the Sierra Maestra.

with operations of the guerrilla forces in the mountains. By this time, the Second Front of the Escambray and the Revolutionary Directorate were active in our province. The group, organized by members of the Popular Socialist Party (PSP),* was active in Jobo Rosado, Yaguajay. It was led by Regino Machado. Members of the Authentic Party and July 26 Movement joined this group and we also provided them with resources.

Preparations for the April 9, 1958, general strike were coordinated by the national leadership of the movement. In the initial phase, it was my role to inform the municipal leaders of the mobilization, and not everyone was receptive to the idea. This reaction was understandable considering the difficulties and errors made in preparing the strike. These errors, along with the mistakes made at the heroic action at Sagua la Grande, were later acknowledged.

It was a different situation in Cienfuegos, where combatants, demoralized by the failure of the September 5 uprising the previous year, refused to participate unless they received sufficient weapons. Unfortunately, they were proven to be correct. The arms offered from Santa Clara did not arrive in time and were hardly used in the uprising in Cienfuegos. The most regrettable incident occurred when the combatants in Sagua had to retreat under indiscriminate enemy air force bombardment. Many lives were lost as young people were massacred trying to escape.

This terrible blow shook up the organization throughout the entire country, and as a result the movement was reorganized. The national leadership was assumed by Fidel's group in the Sierra Maestra and Fidel became commander-in-chief of all the revolutionary forces, including the militias and the different secretariats of the movement. His prestige and authority were now consolidated.

---

* The People's Socialist Party (PSP) was the former Cuban communist party.

In assessing the causes of the failure of the April 9 strike, clear differences were revealed within the movement regarding tactics and strategy, and on how the struggle against the dictatorship should proceed. Conflicts between the *Sierra* (the guerrillas in the mountains) and the *Llano* (literally: the plain, i.e. the urban underground) arose in almost every decision that was made. Due to a general lack of coordination and structure, the movement was not able to mobilize in towns throughout the country. We lost valuable cadres, among them Marcelo Salado, chief of action and sabotage, and others who gave their lives for the revolution.

As a combatant in the underground struggle, I can say we had many valuable compañeros, who selflessly and repeatedly risked everything. Our work in the towns was very difficult, especially as we never knew who might betray us. The repressive forces did not discriminate on grounds of sex, age or rank. From my experience as a guerrilla, I am convinced that both forms of struggle are necessary, each having an equally important role, independent of whatever errors might be made.

After the strike of April 9 and the subsequent reorganization of the movement, some combatants had to leave and others went into hiding. The provincial leadership ordered me to seek refuge in the Teachers Clinic for eight days until things had calmed down a bit. When we recommenced our activity, we were faced with an ever more ruthless enemy. Members of my own family became victims of the regime's violent repression; my cousin Laureano Anoceto March and his son Eduardo Anoceto Rega were tortured and assassinated in the aftermath of the April 9 strike.

I continued in my role as the point of contact, a task I carried out along with Diego Paneque, a member of the provincial leadership and head of action and sabotage. Our compañeros were really like our brothers and sisters so it pains me to recall how some like Diego, whom I saw as a loyal, valiant man who had shown great courage, later found it difficult to adapt to the changes and abandoned the revolution.

We continued our contact with other guerrilla groups active in Corralillo, Santo Domingo, San Diego, La Esperanza and Yaguajay. I visited one of the groups located in San Diego in May. It was there I had my first experience of being bombed by aircraft. I hid under a guásima, a native tree. I can't describe how terrified I was. We returned to La Esperanza taking extra precautionary measures until we reached Santa Clara.

During the offensive by rebel troops I made other trips. On one of these I saw army tanks heading east to the former province of Oriente. We were in a car transporting arms and provisions. I traveled to Matanzas and Camagüey and I went to Havana for the first time. I remember very little of that trip because I was so focused on the task at hand. That is how we all were: dedicated and focused on what we were doing. Every day the situation became more volatile. The dictatorship was destroying an entire generation of young people. Elections were proposed for November 3, 1958, but this ploy was soundly rejected by the people.

The revolutionary offensive began with the rebels moving down from the mountains, supported by forces in the towns. We knew that victory would not be far off. Having strengthened the foothold in the Sierra Maestra, Fidel ordered the invasion of Oriente in the east, and then a move toward the center of the island, repeating the famed exploits of the *mambisa* armies during the war of independence against Spain. Camilo Cienfuegos, one of the commanders, was selected to lead this perilous mission to move his troop toward Pinar del Río in the west of the island. Meanwhile, Ernesto Che Guevara (now also a commander) had the responsibility to bring together all the forces active in the Escambray Mountains (central Cuba), uniting all the different guerrilla groups including the Revolutionary Directorate, the Second Front of the Escambray, the Authentic organization and the PSP in Yaguajay. Once a united front had been created, Che was to advance and take the main towns, finally reaching Santa Clara, where the enemy's communication with the east of the country would be cut off.

Camilo arrived first on the outskirts of Yaguajay, where he made contact with two guerrilla forces formed by the PSP and the July 26 Movement. Once we received word of his arrival, Diego and I went to their camp. This was my first meeting with the legendary commander. We ate a meal with Camilo and Sergio del Valle in a very pleasant atmosphere; Sergio was the doctor of the column and Camilo's assistant. During this meeting we discussed the best way to move into the southern zone via Aguada. On another occasion I went with Serafín Ruiz de Zárate to establish the necessary support structure for the guerrillas. We stayed in a house where Camilo would often stay and I had to sleep in a bed close to his. I will never forget his nightmares; it seemed as though he was fighting the enemy in his sleep. I found it impossible to sleep that night.

Before the arrival of the commanders Camilo and Che, the situation of the small, isolated guerrilla groups in the center of the island was extremely difficult. I never visited Bordón in Quemados. After the strike of April 9, however, I received an order to bring him to the town of Cienfuegos. He could no longer stay in that area after he had participated in the ambush and execution of Colonel Pedraza's son, who was an agent of the SIM, one of the regime's most repressive organizations. I picked up Bordón at the Washington sugar mill near a cane field close to Sagua and Quemados. Bordón showed me Pedraza's pistol that he had taken from the son. The weapon was dedicated to Trujillo, the dictator from the Dominican Republic. I wouldn't allow him to keep the gun because of the danger it posed as evidence, so we headed for Cienfuegos unarmed. I left Bordón at a clinic in the care of Digna Sires, Ruiz de Zárate and Osvaldo Dorticós, who took him to the mountains.

I carried out a few other similar missions that year in a very dangerous and tense atmosphere. I was already being watched by Batista's forces. They had been to my house to conduct searches on a few occasions. I was lucky to escape by pure chance or through the incompetence of the police — maybe it was both. But it was clear that my days in the underground struggle were numbered.

I carried out one of my last tasks as an underground activist after the fraudulent elections in November 1958. I received the order to go to the Escambray Mountains via Sancti Spiritus with the aim of taking funds to the leadership to help finance the guerrilla struggle. My mission also involved taking Dr. Rodríguez de la Vega to Havana where he was working with a section of Batista's army, which supported the July 26 Movement. We were accompanied, on that occasion, by Marta Lugioyo, Serafín Ruiz de Zárate and Dr. Graciela Piñera, who was going to receive orders and new contacts for actions being planned.

Although this was an important mission, for me it was just another assignment. I knew I would meet the famous commander Che Guevara this time. Che had reached the foothills of the Escambray during October, heading the "Ciro Redondo" Eighth Column, named for the outstanding combatant of the assault on the Moncada barracks, who was killed in combat in the Sierra Maestra. Che was now leading the rebel force invasion of central Cuba. I should not need to stress here that my sole motivation was a desire to complete the task I had been given. I was like any other combatant following orders. I had no expectations beyond that.

Of course, I had heard about the legendary exploits of Ernesto Che Guevara. Stories about him were related almost on a daily basis on the clandestine Radio Rebelde (the rebel radio station). Batista's government had labeled him a communist. "Wanted" photos of him and Camilo Cienfuegos were posted around the streets of Santa Clara. When I eventually met Che, I realized the photo on those posters looked nothing like him.

My journey climbing up the Escambray was most uncomfortable because, in order to avoid being robbed, I couldn't tell anyone I was carrying money, which was taped to my torso. As darkness fell, I found it harder and harder to keep up with the others on our hike to Gavilanes, where Che first set up a camp in the liberated zone of Las Villas. On arrival, I met with Dr. Vincente de la O., the doctor who attended to the wounded. I stayed in the little hospital they had set up but could not remove the adhesive tape I had stuck to my body.

In the morning we set off again, this time on horseback, heading to El Pedrero. By nightfall we reached the guerrilla commander's camp. This was my first close encounter with the much admired troops of the Rebel Army. We were greeted by Oscar Fernández Mell, the doctor of the guerrilla unit, who had come with Che from the Sierra Maestra, as well as Alberto Castellanos, Harry Villegas and others; everyone was trying to get a look at the new faces, especially mine, as I was young and one of the few women to visit — a rare presence in the guerrilla camp. In fact, some of the boldest in the group dared to ask if I was the girlfriend of one of the new arrivals.

Oscarito Fernández Mell showed us around and introduced us to everyone. As was to be expected, Che first met with Rodríguez de la Vega and then Ruiz de Zárate. Ruiz de Zárate had already been in the Escambray until he realized his expertise was not needed there; he then decided to return to his work in the underground struggle in another town.

Finally it was my turn to meet Che. I was standing next to

Marta Lugioyo, a lawyer and member of the movement, who had met Che on a previous visit.

After being introduced to the commander, she took me aside and asked me what I had thought of him. I replied somewhat casually that I thought he wasn't bad, and that I found his penetrating gaze rather intriguing. I saw him as an older man. Marta, on the other hand, commented on his beautiful hands, something I had not noticed at the time, but did later on. After all, we were just two women meeting a rather attractive man.

When I had the opportunity to speak to Che, I told him I had come to deliver a package. The adhesive tape was still giving me terrible pain, and I asked him for help to remove it. So that was our first meeting.

4

The first thing I did when I met Che was explain why I had come to the guerrillas' camp. He responded to my request for help in removing the adhesive tape with which the package was strapped to my waist by asking some of his men to assist me. I noticed, in an instant there were quite a few eager volunteers. Of course, I immediately handed over the 50,000 pesos I had brought. Oscar Fernández Mell (the doctor) was chosen to assist me and attend to my wounds. But that was not the end of my embarrassment. I had also torn my trousers when I mounted my horse. So Oscarito gave me a needle and thread to sew up my trousers in order to meet the leader with a bit more dignity.

Later that night, I was shown where I could sleep—a hammock I thought looked wonderful as I was so tired. But I couldn't sleep. I heard voices, and my curiosity got the better of me. I couldn't resist getting up to observe Che speaking to a compañero, whom I later learned was Sidroc Ramos. Ramos was a member of Che's column, but in the darkness I thought he was a Russian, confirming, in my political ignorance, that Che was indeed a communist. At the time, there were many compañeros in our movement with limited political education who held strong prejudices against communism. I was no exception.

I stayed in the camp for three or four days waiting to leave. I was constantly pestered by various guerrillas trying to chat me up. Nevertheless, my memories of this first contact with the Rebel

Army are happy. I struck up friendships with some compañeros who have remained dear friends, through good times and bad, throughout all these years. One of them, now General Rogelio Acevedo, I thought looked like a young girl the first time I saw him. He had long, blonde hair that blew in the wind; I remember plaiting his hair. I also met *Vaquerito* ("Little Cowboy," Roberto Rodríguez), an amiable and brave young man, who loved to tell stories that made us laugh. There was also Harry Villegas, for whom I have always had a great affection, and many others, who became heroes or martyrs in our struggle.

I felt a bit insecure, having spent so much time as an underground activist. Now, even though I was an experienced combatant, in the mountains I was just another insignificant person expected to follow orders. As it was, I could no longer remain in the city, one of the reasons I had been sent to the Escambray. My new challenge was to become a soldier, at least that was my intention. I planned to propose this to Che when we met to discuss my future.

I met with him one evening and we talked about this. He proposed I stay on in the camp as a nurse. Newcomers were always given a specific task as he didn't allow anyone to just "float." I responded bluntly, explaining that I thought my two years of clandestine work gave me the right to be incorporated into the guerrilla unit. He didn't agree and, as a compromise, said I should return to the city to complete some other important assignments, such as the collection of taxes from the sugar growers.

I went to the nearby town of Placetas, where I was greeted by the co-coordinator of the movement. He suggested I return to the guerrilla camp immediately because a warrant for my arrest had been issued. In my role as the point of contact with the movement leaders in the province, I had information that was extremely sensitive and very useful to the enemy. That was the main reason I returned to the Escambray.

I was in Placetas for about 10 days, waiting for the person who would take me back to Che's camp. I was impatient, not only because I was staying with people I didn't know, whom I might be putting at risk, but also because I wanted to join my compañeros in the struggle.

Years later, Che confessed that, at the time, he thought I had been sent by the leadership of the movement in Las Villas (largely made up of right-wing people), to monitor him because of his reputation as a communist. That was why he was reluctant to let me join the guerrilla unit; moreover, he was unaware that I couldn't return to the city.

After the town of Fomento was captured on December 18, I returned to the mountains. I met with Bordón, who gave me a gun. Someone was sent to retrieve some of my clothes and some toiletries from my home; it was then that I bumped into Fernández Mell and Alberto Castellanos, whom I persuaded to support my decision to stay in the camp. Everyone agreed, except Che.

Che later ordered Olo Pantoja to take me to El Pedrero. I was visibly annoyed and sat in the doorway of one of the local houses, which I later learned was called Manaquitas. After a little while, Ernestina Mazón approached me. She was a nurse, who had gone to the Escambray in October, along with a group of technicians, doctors and other nurses, all members of the July 26 Movement in Santa Clara.

My bad mood was such that I didn't go to bed that night. Everyone tried to find me a job, but I didn't want to do any of those offered. To make matters worse, a compañero was annoying me by confessing his romantic interest in me. This made my situation even more difficult and I wanted to escape from this. I

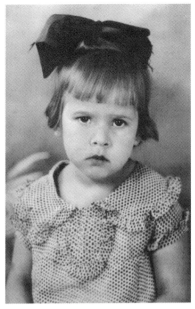

Aleida at the age of five, the only photo of her as a child.

Aleida's parents, Juan March and Eudoxia de la Torre, in front of their house in the country.

Aleida as a teenager.

At her parents' house in the country.

Nombre — Aleida — March de la Torre =

Natural de Santa Clara =

Prov. Las Villas =

Matriculada en primer = curso con el número AB 29 = en las asignaturas que al dorso se expresan.

Santa Clara, —1 DIC 1949

Firma del Alumna

Secretario.

PARA MAESTROS — LAS VILLAS

CARNET DE IDENTIFICACION

NULO SIN EL CUÑO

Firma del Interesado.

Colegio Nacional de Maestros Normales y Equiparados
Colegio Municipal de Santa Clara

CERTIFICAMOS: Que __ la Sr.ta.

Aleida March de la Torre

cuyo retrato y firma aparecen al frente, es miembro del Colegio Municipal de Maestros Normales y Equiparados de Santa Clara y ha llenado los requisitos de inscripción correspondiéndole el No. 816 en el Registro General de Colegiados, habiendo dado cumplimiento a lo dispuesto en la Ley 10 de 21 de Noviembre de 1946 de Colegiación obligatoria de profesionales no universitarios.

Y para constancia, se le expide el presente en Santa Clara, a

13 de Septiembre de 1954

Decano.

Secretario General.

Aleida's student cards from teacher training college.

Aleida playing softball at high school, 1948.

Aleida (left) with classmates at teacher training college, 1953.

On graduating from teacher training college, in 1953. Aleida (front row, second from the right) was elected Queen of the Santa Clara Carnivals.

Graduation ceremony, 1953.

Central University of Las Villas (1955), where Aleida furthered her pedagogical studies (back row, second from the left).

At her friend Mercedes López's home in Rancho Veloz.

Santa Clara aqueduct.

Aleida with her parents and siblings in Santa Clara.

Cabaiguán, after the town of Fomento was captured during the revolutionary war in 1958.

Cabaiguán during the campaign in Las Villas (1958).

Che and Aleida on the way to Caibarién during the campaign in Las Villas (1958).

Che and Camilo Cienfuegos during the capture of El Pedrero.

Aleida and Teresita Orizondo at the command headquarters during the battle of Santa Clara (1958).

Aleida with Che at the National Radio station in Placetas.

Che, after troops from his Column 8 blew up Falcón Bridge.

In the barracks during the capture of Remedios.

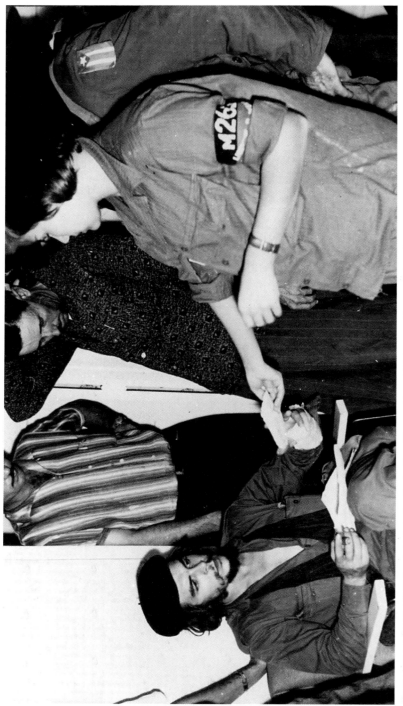

Above Buena Nueva shop in a break during the battle of Santa Clara (1958).

In front of the armored train that was derailed in Santa Clara on December 29, 1958.
(Photo taken by Che.)

Entering the city of Santa Clara in December 1958. "A very young Chinese photographer appeared, camera in hand. Thanks to him, this moment was preserved for posterity."

The surrender of the Leoncio Vidal Regiment's barracks.

could always count on my compañeros, like my friend Ernestina, who knew I had won the right to be integrated as a combatant in the guerrilla troop.

The July 26 Movement announced the formation of a provisional government in Fomento. One day soon after that, Che turned up in El Pedrero at around dawn, and from that moment our common story begins.

I was sitting in the street holding my travel bag on my knees when Che passed by in a jeep and invited me to come along with him "to shoot a few rounds." Without a second thought, I accepted and jumped into his jeep. And that was it. In a way, I never again got out of that jeep.

In any case, we really never had time to stop and think what might happen. Che was at the wheel and I jumped in beside him, instinctively sitting close to him, seeking his protection. At that time, I saw him as someone much older than I, who would protect me from the advances of other compañeros. There were some incidents, such as the time three men were sitting behind me in the back of the jeep. I should say those three men (Harry Villegas, Alberto Castellanos and Jesus Parra) have remained among my closest friends. One of them—I don't know who—touched my back as a bit of a joke; I reacted so violently they never attempted to touch me again.

After Che's spontaneous invitation, there was no time to think about what this might mean on a personal level. I was committed to a cause I was confident would win. There were difficult and memorable moments, and there were also very painful times, but I remained optimistic and confident in the future. In spite of everything, I was blissfully happy at that time.

5

Gradually, as the days passed, I became less in awe of Che's "reputation," and instead developed a tremendous admiration and respect for him. He was very intelligent and had an ability to lead others. He exuded a sense of security and confidence that made the troops he led feel supported at all times, even in difficult circumstances. He had no qualms in facing an enemy with vastly superior strength, and besides his incredible courage, the guerrillas could count on a leader with an extraordinary sense of tactics and strategy.

Events developed at hurricane speed. This left little time for reflection beyond the immediate exigencies of the war. We became machines focused almost exclusively on combat. We had the advantage of being led by a man who erased any doubts, inspiring us with his unwavering support and confidence. My admiration for Che transcended even the bounds of my growing romantic attachment to him.

After capturing Fomento, Che proposed we take Cabaiguán. So that is where we headed. From a farm just outside the town, we could see a camp of soldiers. A couple of scouts were sent off to check it out. We then continued our march into the town where we found no soldiers. We stayed in a tobacco factory on the edge of town; in preparing for a battle, we established our headquarters and radio communication base there. Che chose this tense moment to recite a poem to me. This was one of the most beautiful ways he knew to express himself.

I was standing in the doorway of the factory and suddenly, from behind, Che started to recite a poem I didn't know. Because I was chatting with others at the time, this was his way of attracting my attention. I suspected he wanted me to notice him, not as a leader or my superior but as a man. The more time we spent together, I could feel the sparks between us.

As part of the guerrilla unit, I slowly overcame any doubts that I could be a useful member of the troop. I took the opportunity to go to a friend's house and have a shower. There I was asked, as everyone did, what I thought of Che. I responded as I had to Marta: that he was an older man, very serious, and had a lot of authority. I was only in my early twenties and Che appeared to me much older than he actually was. In reality, he was just 30 at that time.

When we returned to the command post, to my surprise I saw he had his left arm in a cast. During the battle to capture the barracks he had fractured his arm when he had tried to jump over a fence. I gave him a black gauze scarf I had to use as a sling. Over the years, that scarf came to symbolize so much for us. In one of the sweetest things he ever wrote to me, he mentions that scarf. While he was in the Congo, he wrote a short story for me called "The Stone." In his characteristic ironic, subtle style, he remembers the gauze scarf "she gave me in case I injured my arm…"* But that was a long way in the future, after we had experienced much together….

After I got over my initial fright at seeing him wounded, my reaction was to scold him for not waiting for me. I knew the streets of Cabaiguán well and I was sure I could have chosen a safer route into town. From that moment, I was determined to never leave his side under any circumstance so that I could protect him. I thought if I was beside him, he would be safe.

---

* Che's short story, "The Stone," is included as an appendix to this book.

Meanwhile, the battle raged with Che leading what was initially a small guerrilla unit; one of the army snipers who had killed one of our members was shot. The enemy surrendered and Cabaiguán was liberated on December 23. That same day the town of Guayos also fell to the rebels.

The focus of the war then shifted to Placetas, and we immediately transferred there. At first, we stayed in a food supply store in that town, huddling between sacks of grain to protect ourselves from aircraft bombing raids. At a nearby house Che spoke with Rolando Cubela and Juan Abrahantes, combatants of the Revolutionary Directorate located on the outskirts of town. Later on I dared to ask Che about this meeting, despite my respect for him and the fact that this might be considered speaking out of turn. He told me that he had made the commitment to give them a third of our weapons in order to maintain unity among the rebel forces. I understood then that his response showed the level of trust as political confidants that now existed between us.

We made our way to Las Tullerías hotel where, with remarkable energy, Che threw himself into preparing for what later became one of his biggest military feats, the battle of Santa Clara. He gave me instructions to copy the passwords to be sent to Sinecio Torres in Manicaragua. From then on, I acted as Che's personal assistant, which meant I was hardly engaged in any combat but was always at his side. We traveled by jeep to Remedios; I sat in the middle as I usually did. The orders were clear. We were to burn the town council building because the government forces would not surrender. Perhaps Che didn't fully understand the significance of this act as we Cubans did. For us it was reminiscent of the heroic fire at Bayamo in 1868, when our struggle for independence began. The people of Bayamo chose to burn down their town rather than give it up to the Spanish colonialists, an action that revived the dream of true independence.

The army barracks at Placetas surrendered. We came in from behind the barracks and saw a rebel soldier sitting on a bench in the garden, sweating and anxious. When Che asked him why he was sitting there, the soldier told him he had lost his weapon. Che ordered him to continue fighting in order to obtain a new weapon. I thought this a very harsh order, but I also had to acknowledge I was still being initiated into the art of war. Che recalled that young man some years later, in one of the most moving chapters in his *Reminiscences of the Cuban Revolutionary War*. He describes how he found that young soldier who had been wounded in the turmoil of taking the town of Placetas. While offering homage to all those combatants who died in combat, in this piece Che also reflects on the conflict he felt as a leader, having to be so strict and inflexible with his men, becoming someone almost devoid of human feelings. In a way, Che was criticizing himself, while recognizing the difficult situation, revealing himself as someone who was conscious of what he had to do even though he might regret the outcome.

I remember an episode that highlights the spirit of our forces in those final days. I had admonished a compañero because he was sleeping in the midst of battle. He replied that he had been disarmed for accidentally firing his weapon. I responded with habitual dryness, "Get yourself another rifle by going disarmed to the front line… if you're up to it." In Santa Clara, while speaking to the wounded in the Sangre Hospital, a dying man touched my hand and said, "Remember, commander? In Remedios you sent me to find a weapon… and I earned it here." He was the combatant who had accidentally fired his weapon. He died a few minutes later, probably content for having proven his courage. Such was our Rebel Army.*

---

* See "The Final Offensive and the Battle of Santa Clara," in Ernesto Che Guevara: *Reminiscences of the Cuban Revolutionary War* (Seven Stories Press, 2025).

There is a photo of those crazy days that captures a moment in which I was showing Che a piece of soap and everything that symbolized. At the time the guerrillas had no time to sleep or eat, let alone wash. He was unfazed, given that we had to leave immediately for Caibarién, which had been attacked during the night of December 25. We could think of nothing but combat. We couldn't focus on feeling tired, hungry or sleepy. Exhaustion and hunger were our constant companions until the end of the war. That is how it was.

Upon reaching Caibarién we met up with *Vaquerito*, the head of the troop's "suicide squad." He informed Che that he had closed off the road. Che reprimanded him and told him to dismantle the barricade. I couldn't restrain another "intrusion." I whispered to Che that he himself had ordered the barricade be set up, but perhaps had been half asleep when he had done so. To my surprise he responded in a calm tone saying, yes, I was right.

I sometimes think that this really cemented the bond between us. Che came to respect my forthrightness, even if I might be reprimanded for it. He may not have had a companion with Sancho Panza's wisdom and sagacity but he had one who was loyal and constant.

The capture of Caibarién was different from other towns because it was close to the sea and there was a frigate off-shore that had to be neutralized. The crew did not give up until the army barracks had surrendered. I thought the confrontation would last longer than it did, but luckily it didn't. *Vaquerito* played a key role in this, as did his "suicide squad."

We returned to Las Tullerías hotel in Placetas, which had become our command post in that town. There we had our first meeting with Antonio Núñez Jiménez, a geographer and university professor, a member of the PSP who collaborated with the July 26 Movement. He had come at Che's request so we would have a cartographer's assistance in the final preparations for the capture of Santa Clara. He was planning the best direction from which to attack the town. Based on the information we had, it was decided we should enter from La Vallita, located between Santa Clara and Placetas. We would avoid the central highway, which was now blocked because the Falcon Bridge had been destroyed in an action carried out by the rebels of Che's Eighth Column in the first days of December. On that occasion the guerrilla troop had been led by Captain Manuel Hernández, who years later accompanied Che to Bolivia using the *nom de guerre* Miguel. There was an amusing anecdote about the destruction of the Falcon Bridge. When Che heard about the action, he went to check the bridge. It was only just standing; and when he touched it with his foot, the bridge collapsed. That was all it took for Che's men to tease him saying he had destroyed the bridge with a single kick.

On December 26, Che and I were returning quite exhausted from Cabaiguán. We had spent practically eight days without eating or sleeping. We drank some malt beer, the first real nourishment we had for days. It was so good that I can still taste it even now. We went to meet Ramiro Valdés. Che gave him instructions, insisting that the town be handed over to the civil authority of the July 26 Movement. Attending this meeting were Allán Rosell (the coordinator of the movement in the province in 1957) and other combatants from the column, including San Luis (Eliseo Reyes) and Olo Pantoja, who were both recovering from wounds received in the battle for Guayos. These last two compañeros also fought (and died) with Che in Bolivia.

Despite the fact that most of the combatants were not yet aware of the overall strategy, that meeting was to clarify our tactics. Ramirito Valdés would head east to Jatibonico; Bordón and Chaviano would stay close to the town on the central highway from Cienfuegos, after destroying the bridge over the Sagua River to stop reinforcements coming from Matanzas. Che would go to Placetas to prepare for the offensive in Santa Clara. The rest of the men of his Eighth Column were waiting in Placetas, along with forces of the Revolutionary Directorate, to finalize details of the attack.

We left the town in a jeep on the night of December 27, arriving at the university in the early hours of December 28. As usual, I traveled with the bodyguards, this time without Parritas, who had stayed behind in Placetas. Ramirito drove the jeep and would then go on to carry out the mission he had been given. The most wonderful thing about that trip was that we shared a large can of peaches. I have no idea where it came from but those peaches tasted like nectar of the gods.

Our first command post in Santa Clara was set up at the Central University within a couple of hours. It would later be moved closer into town. That morning I was overwhelmed when, quite unexpectedly, Che gave me an M-1 rifle, saying that I had earned it. This was my first important achievement as a combatant; I was keenly aware of how strict Che was in his criteria for who should receive weapons. I felt very satisfied and extremely proud.

We got the news that the group led by Acevedo and Alberto Fernández had already reached Santa Clara and had explored the various routes leading into town. They had already been able to speak to some local people.

On the morning of December 28, the rest of the troops began to advance along the road from Camajuaní and this led to the first clash with enemy soldiers. Batista's tanks were hidden in the surrounding areas. We suffered a few losses: four seriously injured were taken to my old school of pedagogy at the Central University, now converted into a war hospital. This was the moment Che saw the young man from Remedios, the same man he had ordered to find a weapon to replace the one he had lost.

The young man was now mortally wounded. Che took his hand and spoke to him briefly; he was very moved by this encounter. Deeply saddened, he left Oscarito to care for the poor guy, knowing nothing more could be done for him. I didn't have the courage to enter the hospital as I knew that the compañeros inside were in a bad state.

A little while later we took the jeep to Camajuaní, very close to the outskirts of Santa Clara, in order to check out the situation for ourselves. We immediately saw some snipers on Capiro Hill. Luckily, the tanks had retreated, suggesting that the army's morale was quite low, in contrast to the fame that preceded Che everywhere he went. At this point, we were approached by Luis Lavandeiro, a man of French origin, armed with a .30-caliber machine gun. He was accompanied by a group of rebels from the army recruits school. When they heard gunfire from a small plane that was bombing the town, they retreated.

Che responded immediately, ordering the troops to stay and fight. He grabbed a machine gun and started firing. More than anything, his action was symbolic, but it helped overcome the panic. He knew that a .30-caliber machine gun would have minimal impact against the bombardment from an enemy plane. In the confusion of the battle, I thought Che's attitude was crazy and that he had failed to realize we faced a stronger, better-equipped enemy supported by aircraft. I doubted our chance of victory and thought we would have to retreat. Everything happened so quickly that there was no time to speculate and we continued to advance. I was afraid Che would be hurt at any moment, which luckily did not happen, but I overcame my fear and hesitation, focusing on the battle we had to win. Che had already proven himself to be an exceptional leader, and he did this again in Santa Clara.

We headed into the town, coincidentally passing by the house belonging to Lolita Rosell, a friend from the urban underground. By this time, it was December 28, the day of the Innocent Saints,* and everyone was playing pranks. When I saw the look of confusion on my friend's face, I told her she was not hallucinating, but that our dream was becoming reality. We continued to the Public Works building and set up the second command post, where orders were given for the final offensive.

That afternoon we returned with the bodyguards by jeep to El Pedrero, which was now totally secure. We attended the funeral of a combatant. We also visited José Ramón Silva, one of our captains who had been badly wounded in Cabaiguán. On our return we visited Leonardo Tamayo (Tamayito), also wounded, but not as seriously. We met up with my friend Ernestina, a nurse for the column, and Che asked her to look after Silva, who was in a critical state.

On our way back, at sunset, something most unexpected happened. I don't know if it was because of the time of day, or because of a deep need he had, but for the first time Che spoke to me about his personal life. He told me about his marriage to Hilda Gadea (a Peruvian economist), and his daughter, Hildita. At the time I wasn't sure if he had said Hildita was three or 13 years old. He told me that by the time he left Mexico he had already separated from Hilda. He told me of their many misunderstandings and, from the way that he spoke about her, I sensed he no longer loved her, or at least he wasn't in love with her. I couldn't really figure out what he was trying to tell me in this conversation, but I was more inclined to take Hilda's side, because of my tendency to defend other women. In fact, he was trying to tell me he was no longer married and was struggling to express his feelings. I was still under the sway of my romantic novels, and was also involved in the struggle for the freedom of

---

* December 28 is the equivalent of April Fool's Day (April 1) in Latin America.

both my country and myself. I imagined Hilda as a very elegant woman with a strong personality. It couldn't be any other way because how could such a courageous and virile man not have that type of woman at his side? Despite my romantic notions, at that time Che appeared to be very much alone. I could not begin to imagine how much his commitment was based on love.* But sensing this brought me closer to the commander who was leading such an important battle. It also brought me closer to the man.

I can see myself in that car in the fading afternoon light, in the company of a man who is relating the story of his life to a fellow soldier. She, aware of what is going on around her, is looking out for the safety of her commander. But Che is interrupted and we continue on our way.

During the actions that took place in Cabaiguán and Placetas, we traveled by jeep to see Camilo Cienfuegos in Yaguajay. We had some most enjoyable times within the maelstrom of the war, and those moments brought us all closer together. They helped us get to know each other as we really were. Some of us were naïve, others, very clever; we were all young and full of hope for a future victory. We took every chance to have fun. I remember one day when we were traveling in the jeep with Oscarito, Nuñez and his wife, Lupe Velis. Alberto Castellanos was at the wheel and I suddenly realized that everyone was falling asleep, including Alberto. I began to chat with him so that he wouldn't fall asleep, describing all the beautiful places in Cuba, like the beach at Varadero. He fancied himself as a bit of a lady's man, so with his characteristic cheeky grin he remarked that the best thing at the beach were the women. He sighed when he mentioned a particular beach in Holguín, Guardalavaca. Then he

---

* Che later wrote: "At the risk of seeming ridiculous, let me say that the true revolutionary is guided by a great feeling of love. It is impossible to think of a genuine revolutionary lacking this quality."

sighed, "Oh what women!" These were our compañeros: simple folk, sometimes crude, but always full of respect and affection for their compañeros. Our joking woke all the others and in the midst of the hilarity we hit a pothole in the road. We arrived at our destination a little late but in a very jolly mood. At the end of the day Camilo showed us his famous "war tank," baptized with the impressive name of "Dragon," a name that quite contradicted its rather rudimentary design.

At around this time, on Che's orders I went on a mission with Harry Villegas. As we approached the command post on our return, we saw B-26s flying overhead, releasing their bombs indiscriminately on the defenseless population. I had Che's camera and my M-1 rifle with me. Instinctively, I dropped to the ground to protect myself, even though Villegas was trying to tell me there was no danger. In my fall, I broke the camera, something I regarded as a disaster. I asked Villegas not to tell Che how the camera came to be broken and he respected my request. Friendships and mutual affection, forged during this time, have remained intact to this day.

Arriving exhausted back at the command post at midday, I gave Villegas the camera and lay down on the floor to rest. I was on the verge of tears, thinking when Che found out he would accuse me of cowardice. Thankfully the incident stayed between Villegas and me. But it wasn't the only blunder that might have exposed me in our leader's eyes. On the night of December 29, Che and I went out for a walk along the highway. He scrutinized everything so that no detail escaped him, and I took notes like a good assistant. He told me we had to locate a "Caterpillar," a bulldozer, in order to lift the railroad tracks to derail the dictator's armored train that was expected to arrive.

Che had a deep, guttural voice and because it was late at night he spoke in a whisper. I didn't understand what he had said. I had no idea what a Caterpillar was—he used the word "Caterpillar" in

English—so I noted down what I thought he had said in Spanish: "*catres, palas y pilas*" [beds, shovels and batteries]. It was a mistake on my part and, realizing I was confused, he asked to see what I had written. He jokingly remarked, "A teacher, eh?" Dreadfully embarrassed, I answered defensively, "What do you expect? I don't know what a 'Caterpillar' is." I couldn't hide my shame, so I remained silent. From that moment on, every time something similar happened he would sarcastically remind me of this. Years later, when I told our children this story, they enjoyed taunting me, chanting: "Beds, shovels and batteries!"

In spite of my ignorance, a Caterpillar miraculously appeared in the morning, driven by a civilian with instructions to raise the tracks. When he set about doing this, he was shot at. Another older man, who was an innocent bystander, was shot in the stomach and had to be taken to the clinic nearby. With the aid of a telescope, we tried to see where the shots were coming from. We realized there were black figures moving on the roof of the Gran Hotel (now the Santa Clara Libre Hotel) located across from Vidal Park. From their vantage point, the snipers had a good view of the entire town. Che immediately went to find a member of the "suicide squad," ordering him to lift up the railroad tracks.

This is how, on the afternoon of December 30, the famous armored train was derailed and fell into our hands.

Just after we succeeded in damaging the railroad tracks, Che and I entered Santa Clara, accompanied by Guile (Ramón Pardo Guerra), Harry Villegas and José Argudín. We walked down Independence, the main street. Before we reached Maceo Street we met a young Chinese photographer, who had his camera with him, and thanks to him that moment was preserved for posterity.

We continued walking and a few blocks from the park we heard a tank shooting in the distance. Despite the danger, Che crossed the road in front of an armored car and his beret flew off his head. Argudín had gone down another street toward the park. Seeing the armored car, I froze on the spot. I realized we were close to my house, but it took some seconds for me to snap out of it. I crossed the road to Che, thinking I should not leave him alone since I knew he didn't know his way around my town. I was shocked to see Che return to pick up his beret. To our surprise the armored car retreated, maybe suspecting an ambush. We continued together with no further incidents. Sometime later, in one of our rare private moments, Che confessed that when he had seen me in such danger, he realized how much I meant to him. Of course, that was hardly the ideal moment for such a confession.

After walking quite a way, we decided to go to the Church of St. Carmen to review the situation. The church was across the street from the police station, where some compañeros were posted. We headed to where the armored train had been derailed. We crossed the bridge and Che started to issue orders, directing operations. Once the train had been captured he asked Núñez Jiménez and Alberto Castellanos to take Batista's soldiers to Caibarién to transfer them to the frigate there.

Che always treated the prisoners with absolute respect, according to the norms of the Rebel Army, despite the fact that many of those on the train were members of Colonel Sánchez Mosquera's bloodthirsty unit, responsible for the murder of a large number of *campesinos* in the Sierra Maestra.

The fighting continued as we returned to the command post. The next day, December 30, was an ill-fated day. We headed out again on the Maleza highway to go around the train station from where we could reach the police headquarters. Che realized snipers were shooting close to his feet. No one was following him. In a fraction of a second I had rushed to him, as did Fernández Mell. We skirted the old teacher's college, turning into a street where *Vaquerito* ordered us to hide between some houses and to keep out of the way of our combatants, who were advancing towards the snipers. *Vaquerito* ducked across from the station into a gap between the buildings, but he was mortally wounded. With his long hair dripping blood, he was carried by four compañeros. I remember so clearly how paralyzed we were at the sight. Che examined him and told Oscarito to take him straight to the clinic. I asked Che if he was dying because the poor young man was having convulsions. He responded sadly, yes. When Che saw *Vaquerito* so badly wounded, he apparently remarked that his death was equal to that of 100 men. I didn't hear him say this, but that was certainly how we all felt. Everyone regarded him as an exemplary fighter, one who had risked his life many times but who wouldn't live to see the triumph now so close.

Che and I returned to where *Vaquerito* had been killed. He looked around and gave precise orders in the hope of blocking any further action from the enemy. Acevedo attacked the prison and the court house; Alberto Fernández and Alfonso Zayas fought from the cinema Cloris located near the Gran Hotel, where we knew there were enemy forces. Within a few days (December 29-31), with lightning attacks, we derailed the armored train, and took over the provincial government building, the Caballitos barracks of the motorized police, the barracks of the 31st Squadron, the prison and the police station. But we had yet to defeat the enemy troops resisting from the court house, the Gran Hotel and the Leoncio Vidal Regiment's barracks.

Between December 31 and January 1 we attacked the Gran Hotel where I was terrified Che would be wounded. Everything happened so quickly. We rode in tanks we had seized from the police station and we headed to the center of the town where soldiers of the SIM were. We positioned ourselves between the hotel and the park. I had never been inside a tank before and I felt like I was suffocating.

Che got out of the tank and looked around. As he went up the stairs of the Gran Hotel, he realized that there was a grenade on one of the steps. He searched for another way out and somehow managed to reach a tower on the third floor. Meanwhile Villegas and I were sitting in the cinema, waiting for orders from Che. I'm terribly ashamed to say this but, in the darkness of the cinema, for a few minutes we both fell asleep. We fell asleep! Che found us after the enemy had surrendered. The prisoners were locked up in the basement of our command post, and we followed Che, not daring to say a word.

There were many ghastly, hellish incidents in these final moments of the battle of Santa Clara. When Acevedo was attacking the court house he was horrified to see enemy tanks run over one of their own soldiers, who had fallen in combat.

At the command post, our compañera Marta Lugioyo, a lawyer, read out the execution orders, and the names of those who would be executed for committing atrocities. This sentence wasn't carried out, however, because some of the guilty had escaped.

By January 1, Batista had fled Havana, but the Leoncio Vidal Regiment in Santa Clara still had not surrendered. In order to avoid unnecessary bloodshed, Che sent Dr. Rodríguez de la Vega, Núñez Jiménez and Dr. Ruiz de Zárate to negotiate with Colonel Hernández, the head of the regiment. He was warned that if his troops did not surrender by 12:30 the battle would commence. He did not agree.

Once the deadline had passed, the colonel sent Commander Fernández to speak with Che. The ultimatum was repeated and Colonel Hernández was told he would bear full responsibility for whatever happened. There could be no doubt, if it came to a battle, there would be a great many casualties because the forces were disproportionate. The rebels had about 340 men against 3,000 soldiers who, although demoralized, might decide to fight when faced with the prospect of certain death. Fortunately, the enemy eventually surrendered and accepted the revolutionary command's word of honor that their lives would be spared.

On January 1, Che was able to communicate with Fidel via radio, receiving the order to proceed immediately to Havana. Batista and his closest collaborators had fled the evening before and the situation was becoming quite confused. That is why Camilo Cienfuegos was ordered to take his "Antonio Maceo" Second Column to Camp Columbia in Havana, Batista's most important fortress. Che's "Ciro Redondo" Eighth Column went to seize La Cabaña Fortress at the entrance to Havana Bay, which controlled access to the port and the city.

It is difficult to recall exactly everything that happened next. I know that on January 2, before leaving Santa Clara, I went to inspect the Leoncio Vidal Regiment's barracks with Che. Sometime on that day I went to my house to see my parents and collect a few belongings. I told them I was going to Havana because the war was not yet over. My parents were very happy to see me and extremely relieved I had not been injured in all the fighting. They had been very worried after they heard from Marta or Lolita that I had become involved in the armed conflict. To their relief their prodigal daughter had returned unharmed. For the time being they had to be content with a fond farewell. I also had a chance to say good-bye to Lolita. I quickly made my way back to the command post. I was very tired, but at least I had had a chance to have a bath and to find slightly more appropriate clothes. I have to confess that, in the mad rush to leave for Havana, my fear was that I would be left behind. All I wanted to do was to continue with the rebel forces.

When I got back everything was bustling as they prepared to leave for Havana. We went to the regiment's barracks where the Rebel Army command was organizing the troop that would proceed to Havana. We set out on the afternoon of January 2. On the outskirts of Santa Clara, we saw trucks with rebels piled on board. We were in the jeep with our regular compañeros: Alberto, Villegas, Argudín and Hermes Peña. Behind us, in another car, were Rodríguez de la Vega, Núñez Jiménez and others—I can't remember all of them. What had been a dream seemed to have become reality.

6

Every time I try to recall that trip to Havana, the events get jumbled in my mind. I remember feeling all kinds of emotions, partly due to a lack of sleep. I was utterly exhausted, but it was more than that—I think I was now absorbing all the disturbing experiences of recent days and weeks. Whatever the case, I had now embarked on a particular road and I had no doubt it was the right course. It was a time of tremendous expectations and heightened emotions. Leaving Santa Clara in that impromptu convoy, I left behind many of my youthful dreams, although some were now becoming reality.

We made our first stop to refuel at dusk. I think this was in Los Arabos, but it might have been Coliseo. It was a place I knew, having passed through there during my time in the clandestine struggle. But what I could never have imagined was that this place would become so special to me for the rest of my life. In that small, apparently insignificant town, Che first declared his love for me.

We found ourselves sitting alone in the vehicle. He suddenly turned to me and told me he had realized he loved me that day in Santa Clara when the armored car suddenly came up behind us. He said he was dreadfully afraid that something might happen to me. I was exhausted and half asleep, so I was hardly listening to what he was saying. I didn't even take it very seriously, as I still saw him as much older than I was. I had previously had professions of love from others. Moreover, he was my leader, someone I respected and admired. He might have expected some kind of response from me, but at that moment I couldn't utter a word—I was so tired. Also, I thought perhaps I hadn't heard him correctly and I didn't want a repeat of the "Caterpillar" incident.

Looking back, I think Che didn't exactly choose the best moment to declare his love, and I felt a bit upset later thinking he didn't get the response he might have hoped for. But that was it. The others piled back into the jeep, and we were soon on our way again. But the ice had certainly been broken.

We stopped in the town of Matanzas that night. We met up with some of Camilo's troops, and I recall us having something to eat. Che called Camilo from the old telephone company. Camilo was already at Camp Columbia in Havana, and they were able to update one another about the situation. The next day we set off again. A small group of Che's Eighth Column led by Víctor Bordón had gone ahead with Camilo's men, and another group stayed at the Matanzas regiment, under Julio Chaviano's command, in order to maintain order. This was Che's reason for passing through Matanzas on the way to Havana. A few days later, Chaviano joined us in Havana to report to Che about the situation in Matanzas.

Some of us still debate what happened on the next part of the trip to Havana, probably because most of us were from the country and not familiar with the route. My memory is that we stayed on the main highway, and we came into Havana via Cotorro, on the port road and through the tunnel near the bay.

We reached La Cabaña Fortress in the early morning hours of January 3. The head of the fort (Colonel Manuel Varela Castro) was waiting for us. He belonged to the group known as the "pure soldiers" that included José Ramón Fernández and others— soldiers who had been won over to supporting the revolution. Che was told about the unarmed troops stationed at the barracks and he decided not to go there. He went instead to the Military Club, where the non-commissioned officers and prisoners were being held. The officers still had their handguns.

As we made our way to the old army headquarters, there was an eerie calm about the city. After some discussion, we went to the army commander's house in La Cabaña, where we met Lieutenant-Colonel Fernández Miranda (Batista's brother-in-law) and several other high-profile Batista men.

What took place there was quite surreal. It was strange to be in such an enormous fort, watching the soldiers subordinate themselves to the rebel command. This revealed the low morale of Batista's army. More importantly, it showed the trust in and respect for the new Rebel Army, which had proved it had the unconditional support of the Cuban people.

Che and others set up their command post in Fernández Miranda's house, and we stayed the night there. Most of the men slept in the main room, while I was given the smallest separate room. I slept only a few hours as we still couldn't allow ourselves much time to rest. A few of the women with us searched for a change of clothes among Fernández Miranda's wife's things. That morning Che set himself up to work in a small office in the house, but later transferred his office to the army headquarters within the fort. Walking around La Cabaña, we were in awe of the magnificent gardens and the view of the sea, marvelling at the incredible beauty of the place. We, the dispossessed, for the first time felt ourselves masters of our own destiny. But, as Che had always warned, from that moment the real revolutionary struggle would begin.

⊗

A new life began for all of us. The initial chaos gave way to order, and we took the first steps in organizing ourselves, occupying other houses within the fort. On January 5 we took a plane to Camagüey. I had no idea where we were going and even less who we would meet there. During the trip Che dictated some notes to me about the duties of a rebel soldier. This is how I began my first job with him, without it ever being officially decided. Che was aware of the need to jot down his thoughts to assist the process of the revolutionary transformation that had begun.

I stayed in the airport with Commander Manuel Piñeiro (*Barbarroja*)* and Demetrio Montseny (*Villa*), and then we later returned to Havana with Che. The purpose of the trip, as I later discovered, was to meet with Fidel, who was coming in a triumphant cavalcade from Santiago to Havana. They discussed the next steps to be taken and what new orders should be issued. This meeting at the Camagüey airport was captured in a famous photograph that shows both men in a happy, relaxed mood.

A few days later, on January 7, we traveled by car to Matanzas, where Che again met with Fidel. I waited nearby and I met Celia Sánchez** for the first time, and later that day Che introduced me to Fidel. I wanted to say so much to him, but somehow the words abandoned me. I wanted to say how much it meant to meet him and how I felt as though I had known him for a long time. He was the reason I felt my life had a purpose and meaning. I had so much to thank him for, not only because of what had happened historically, but also because if it hadn't been for him I would never have met Che.

We returned to Havana that same day to wait for Fidel. On January 8 from our vantage point on the walls of La Cabaña Fortress,

---

* Manuel Piñeiro (*Barbarroja* or Red Beard) was head of the organization responsible for coordinating Cuba's assistance to liberation and revolutionary movements in Latin America and elsewhere.

** Celia Sánchez was a member of the Rebel Army's general staff and Fidel Castro's personal assistant.

we watched Fidel arrive in Havana. Looking across the bay we could see the huge throng of people crowding around the rebels.

Gradually a certain measure of order was established, despite the excitement and turbulence of the revolution. I, too, began to create some kind of order in my personal life and to adapt to my new life in Havana.

I had to start to do normal, everyday things, or at least try to lead a normal life. I decided to abandon my guerrilla fatigues and dress like a woman. I went with Lupe (Núñez Jiménez' wife) to her mother-in-law's house. She was a dressmaker and she made me a pretty, fashionable dress. Lupe and I also went to the hairdresser together. I soon began to feel like my old self again. We walked around central Havana, acquainting ourselves with the beautiful parts of our capital city for the first time.

Che's bodyguards accompanied him everywhere, on his way to work or if he and I took a stroll together along the Malecón, Havana's famous sea wall. Neither of us knew our way around the city. We would often get lost or stop at a red light thinking it was a traffic light, only to realize it was the light of a pharmacy. We laughed a lot about this, paraphrasing the title of a film by referring to ourselves as the "*campesinos* in Havana."* We were simply two people in love, ruled by our feelings. Sometimes, if he was driving the car, he would ask me to fix the collar of his shirt or he would tell me his arm still hurt so could I fix his hair—these were his sly ways of getting me to caress him in public before we were married.

We lived every minute to the utmost. My friends from the Presbyterian Church invited me a couple of times to attend church with them. Once Che drove me to church in his car, and left me at the door, saying he would pick me up an hour later. I had a wonderful reunion with my old friends Faustino Pérez, Orestes

---

* A reference to a popular movie at the time, "Vampires in Havana."

González, Sergio Arce (who had been my pastor in Santa Clara) and the widow of Marcelo Salado. Che always respected my opinions and told me what he thought. Over time, with the impact of the social transformation taking place around me, and under Che's influence, my attitude to religion changed.

I can't recall who picked me up from the church that time. It was probably one of the bodyguards, and we then went to pick up Che from Ciudad Libertad, as Camp Columbia was now called. In those first days we spent quite a few nights there with Camilo. At other times, Camilo would come across to La Cabaña. Camilo had a reputation as a ladies man. One day he stopped by when Che wasn't around and put me on the spot, bluntly asking me about my relationship with Che. I responded curtly that I was only his secretary. Backing off, he half-jokingly insisted he had only stopped by to see Che, and that was the end of it. Everyone loved Camilo and I took no offense.

La Cabaña Fortress became one of the crucial centers of the revolution, and Che began to emerge as one of the more able and charismatic leaders. The leadership of the new revolutionary government had to be created from a largely illiterate group of former guerrillas, who were not very well prepared for the challenges that lay ahead. Within a few days of Che's arrival, La Cabaña was transformed into a sizable cadre school. Small factories and workshops were established there, similar to those he had organized in the Sierra Maestra. He saw the process of industrialization as an urgent priority for the country. A small magazine called *Cabaña Libre* was produced, promoting discussion of cultural issues. Events were organized at La Cabaña, attended by important national cultural personalities, such as the poet Nicolás Guillén and Carmina Benguría.

The main objective of these activities was the political and cultural development of the Rebel Army soldiers. A great emphasis was placed on literacy classes because the former rebels were often undisciplined and reluctant to study. During the war they had been courageous, an inspiration to others; but they now found it difficult to understand why so much was demanded of them.

This meant an extra burden for Che. Besides the multiple tasks of his daily work, he also committed himself to describing and analyzing the experiences of the revolutionary war in Cuba. He thought such an analysis might offer lessons to other revolutionary movements or national liberation struggles. By this time, Che's talent for military strategy was widely recognized, but nothing was known about his remarkable grasp of revolutionary theory, despite his reputation as a communist.

Che's speech at the cultural society Nuestro Tiempo, a few days after the triumph of the revolution, alerted both friends and enemies to his considerable intellect. In that speech he clearly outlined how he saw the Rebel Army as the vanguard and the source of future cadres for the revolution. As much as time would allow, he analyzed the Cuban revolution from a Marxist perspective—something he would go on to develop in greater detail. This became an important aspect of his legacy.

We all faced a daunting workload. The revolutionary tribunals, organized in January, put on trial those henchmen of the dictatorship who had not succeeded in fleeing with Batista. This was done in conjunction with an investigative commission, presided over by Miguel Angel Duque de Estrada, a lawyer and captain in the Rebel Army.

These tribunals have always been controversial, and the facts about them have often been greatly distorted by our enemies. For Cuba, they were a legitimate form of revolutionary justice, being neither without mercy nor spontaneous. The proper procedures were followed, and I recall that Che participated in some of the appeals, meeting with the families who came to beg for clemency. We adopted a humanitarian approach respectful of the prisoners. Although the process of the tribunals was just, it was, nevertheless, painful and distasteful. Che did not attend the trials nor was he present at any of the executions.

Oscar Fernández Mell, Adolfo Rodríguez de la Vega and Antonio Núñez Jiménez were Che's assistants in La Cabaña. The military intelligence organization was created, and Arnaldo Rivero Alfonso was put in charge of monitoring the behavior of rebel soldiers.

The amount of work I faced was quite overwhelming. I had to attend to the needs and personal problems of the soldiers, according to Che's instructions. I also had to try to control the number of personalities and journalists who came to Havana to interview Che. Among these national and international visitors were Herbert Matthews, Loló de la Torriente and women from many different professions, who sought an audience with Che. My role as Che's personal assistant gained me the rather unjust reputation of being jealous and possessive. I also had to deal with the future girlfriends and wives of Che's assistants and bodyguards.

Former combatants in the underground movement turned up to see for themselves the "communist" who had liberated Las Villas. Others came to see the legendary combatant, who had risked his life for a country not his own, like Máximo Gómez. Gómez was born in the Dominican Republic and came to Cuba to fight in the independence wars against the Spanish. Like Máximo Gómez, Che was declared a Cuban citizen after the revolution.

My temporary office at the residence was also my bedroom. I inherited the previous residents' dog, which for some reason hated soldiers. I never figured out if he only hated our soldiers or if his dislike was more general. Along with the dog, a lot of other things had been left behind, including films of the family of the former military commander of the fort. When we left La Cabaña and moved to Tarará, we took the dog with us, and he remained with us until he died.

I began my role as "treasurer," managing money we still had from the days in the Escambray. I still have those documents and receipts from that time. We maintained strict austerity with regard to our funds. Che ordered a distribution of 10 pesos to each soldier for their holidays.

I also handled Che's personal correspondence. Around January 12 he asked me to read a letter he was sending Hilda (his former wife). He told her they needed an official divorce because he was going to marry a Cuban woman he had met during the struggle. I didn't quite understand his handwriting, so I asked him who was the young woman he intended to marry. He looked at me with surprise and said it was me. The fact is, up until that moment, we had not discussed marriage. Without saying another word I processed the letter. Che's answer surprised me. It wasn't exactly unexpected, but at the same time I wondered why he hadn't ever mentioned this before.

There were other letters, including one he sent to his beloved Aunt Beatriz, which we joked about. This aunt loved Che dearly and idolized her favorite nephew. When he told her he was separating from Hilda and was going to marry me, she wrote somewhat disparagingly about "the girl from the sticks," in a tone that reflected the prejudice of the Argentine oligarchy to which she belonged. It was innocent enough, but demeaning to me. Sometime later, when I met Che's parents at the airport, the first thing Che's father asked him was whether I was "the girl from the sticks."

By that time, our relationship had changed. During January we took a trip to San Antonio de los Banos. This time, we were both sitting in the back seat of the car, and for the first time Che took my hand. Not a word was spoken, but I felt my heart would jump out of my chest. I didn't know what to do or say, but I realized then that there was absolutely no doubt I was in love with him.

Not long after that, on a memorable January night, barefoot and silent, Che came into my room in La Cabaña, and we consummated an already strong relationship. Che jokingly called that day, "the day the fortress was taken." The expression is probably apt because, when you take over a fortress, you must first surround it, determining its weak points, before you decide on the attack. I was even more in love than I knew, so I "surrendered" without resistance.

Everything happened quickly after that. Che's parents arrived on January 18, and we went to meet them at the airport. His father immediately asked who I was, and Che introduced me as the woman he intended to marry. We then went to the hotel where they were staying. It was a very emotional time because from the moment he saw his parents Che exuded happiness. It had been nearly six years since he left his home in Argentina.

During his parents' visit we went to Santa Clara and El Pedrero. That place, where Che had invited me to get into his jeep and "shoot a few shots," marked a decisive moment in my life.

On a personal level, not everything was entirely without difficulty. In the midst of the whirlwind of our lives in these first weeks of the revolution, Hilda arrived. No arrangements had been made for her accommodation. We still lived in the barracks at La Cabaña, with Batista's former soldiers cooking and cleaning for us, and doing other chores around the place. Che was busy learning to fly a plane. Eliseo de la Campa had been his pilot and he owned the plane in which he was teaching Che. Che had planned a trip to the Isle of Pines and, when he heard the news of Hilda's arrival, he came to see me. I was quite ill in bed with rubella. He invited me to join him on his trip. So I immediately got dressed and left with him.

Alberto Castellanos went to collect Hilda at the airport. Che's parents were also waiting for her. When I returned from the trip, Hilda and I were not introduced, but I did manage to catch a glimpse of her. My illusions about her vanished, and my ego was somewhat boosted. In no way could I consider her my rival. I also felt less guilty because it was clear from the letters Che had sent to his family from Mexico (when I wasn't even in the picture) that his relationship with Hilda had ended. We now only had to overcome a few obstacles Hilda had created. These problems were inevitable and, although I was upset at the time, now I can look back much more calmly.

Otherwise, life continued almost normally. We regularly visited the renamed hotel Havana Libre (previously the Havana Hilton), which had become a temporary central headquarters for the rebel troops. On one of those visits, when Che was meeting with Fidel at the hotel, I was waiting in one of the rooms. I was on the bed, chatting to Celia Sánchez and Pastorita Nuñez, when Fidel came in and told me I was in his spot. I was mortified and got up immediately. It was a joke, but at the time I didn't know him well and I thought he was reprimanding me. That room was always packed with people, because many of our compañeros with different responsibilities would go there for meetings and often had to wait patiently for hours. I remember on one occasion I saw Augusto Martínez Sánchez sleeping on the floor while he waited his turn.

Another time, I was sitting on a chair next to the door of that room, and Fidel burst out suddenly with his bodyguards. On seeing me, he stopped for a moment, looked at me and asked — just to be sure — if I was "Che's girl." As you can imagine, I was embarrassed by the question and responded in my usual way saying, no, I was Che's secretary. Sometimes I would say I was his assistant, as I was not in the military, only a former guerrilla. This lack of clarity created a lot of confusion.

During my time at La Cabaña, I received some personal tuition from Armando Hart, our very young, talented Minister for Education. Many people were aware I had completed the final year of my pedagogy course at the Central University in Las Villas. Therefore, Armando decided to honor me with the title of "Doctor of Pedagogy," based on my "practical thesis" on the role of women in society, which I had achieved during the war. I have to admit this gave me much pleasure as I did feel I had earned it.

Many foreigners came to see Che, including a group of Haitians, who came to seek Cuban support for their efforts to overthrow the dictatorial regime of Duvalier. With hindsight I realize that even as early as February 1959 steps were being made to establish Cuba's collaboration with liberation movements and other progressive struggles. I feel privileged to have witnessed this. As a result of those initial conversations with the Haitians, Che sent me to the Sumidero area in Pinar del Río with Hernández López, the captain who later married us in La Cabaña. He was a compañero from the underground struggle in Havana, and had first met Che in Fomento, where he had been sent by the July 26 Movement to work on propaganda. Hernando and his wife, Gloria Pérez, worked with Che until he left for the Congo.

The month of February came around, and so did my birthday. It was not a particularly happy time because Che was already showing symptoms of pulmonary emphysema, as a result of the privations of the war and the pressures of the first, hectic days after the revolution.

My old friend, Lolita Rosell, came by to wish me a happy birthday. I was sitting with Che in his room. She didn't really need to ask; she only had to see us together to sense the intimacy between us.

In the first days of March we moved to a house in Tarará on the beach outside Havana, hoping Che would regain his health in a quieter place and have some respite from his never-ending responsibilities. His bodyguards, whom I always regarded as brothers, came with us. I often had to defend their lack of discipline, and occasionally I was complicit in their nightly escapades. I understood they were young men from the country, many of them from remote villages. They were totally awestruck at being in Havana for the first time — a glittering city of endless nights and beautiful women. They would often sneak out late at night to meet their girlfriends, taking the car. They would roll the car down the hill before starting the engine, so as to leave undetected. Che would ask me if I had heard a noise, probably because he knew what was going on. I would answer, no. I don't think he believed me, but he would let it go at that.

I, too, did some pretty crazy things. I was a terrible driver, only just learning to drive. Roberto Cáceres (*El Patojo* or "Shorty"), a Guatemalan whom Che had met in Mexico, would often accompany me in the car. He had just arrived in Cuba. Tragically, he died some years later fighting for the liberation of his country. They were wild, romantic times. We were young and did things maybe we wouldn't do in other circumstances. We drove around Havana in a huge Oldsmobile, without a clue as to where we were going, but somehow we always arrived at our destination.

We had a lot of fun in those days. Eliseo, Che's pilot, once decided to land his plane in the streets of Tarará, much to everyone's astonishment. I remember them all — Villegas, Hermes Peña, Argudín, Castellanos and others — with deep affection.

The house at Tarará was quite elegant, having previously belonged to a customs officer with links to the dictatorship. After we moved into the house, Che received a malicious letter that was published in the magazine *Carteles*. It asked where the money had come from for such luxurious living, the implication being that it could only be money stolen from the people.

It turned out we only lived in that house for two months and, although it never became much of a home, I have very happy memories of that time. We never had time for a proper rest and we didn't spend a single day at the beach. But it was a wonderful time for Che and me, and was where we were able to achieve a greater sense of intimacy than ever before.

Che gave me his first personal gift there—a bottle of Flor de Roca perfume from Caron. In reality, we didn't have a lot of time to ourselves; compañeros were always coming and going, working on various tasks that couldn't wait. Relatives of those facing execution also came to see Che there. Even the sister-in-law of the former owner of the house showed up, saying she had never been invited there before.

Nevertheless, it was a comfortable house where Che was able to use his bedroom as an office. Being ill, he could remain in bed most of the day when he didn't need to travel to La Cabaña. This gave me a lot of freedom. We breathed a different air; the house had large windows and was well ventilated. It had a small, separate office on the ground floor, and upstairs was Che's large room next to a large bathroom. Because we were not yet married we had to make it appear we slept in separate rooms. So I had my own bedroom. The bodyguards slept in a room at the end of the hall.

There was a large room used for meetings, where many important discussions took place. The first Agrarian Reform Law document was drafted there. There was also a dining room and a modern kitchen, which led to the garage with a small storeroom where the previous owner had stored all kinds of delicacies.

La Cabaña fortress, Havana, January 1959.

A rest break in La Cabaña.

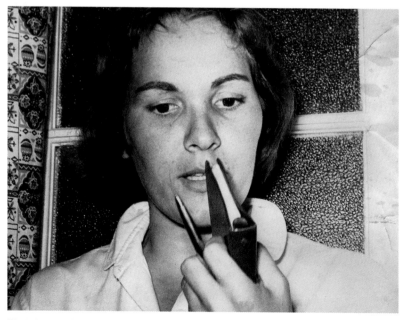

First statements to *Bohemia* magazine, 1959.

Matanzas, January 7, 1959, where Aleida met Fidel Castro for the first time.

In the Presidential Palace, Havana. (Photo taken by Camilo Cienfuegos.)

Trip to El Pedrero with Che's parents.

During a 1959 trip to Sumidero, Pinar del Río, in western Cuba.

Che, Aleida (right), Manuel Piñeiro (left) and others in a parade on May 1, 1959, in Santiago de Cuba.

A trip to Minas del Frío, in the Sierra Maestra mountains.

Che and Aleida, with Vilma Espín (wife of Raúl Castro) and Alejandro, the first Soviet ambassador to Havana, during the visit of Soviet Deputy Prime Minister Anastas Mikoyan

Che and Aleida's wedding, June 2, 1959. From left, Raúl Castro and his wife Vilma Espín.

Che and Aleida's wedding, June 2, 1959.

Che and Aleida's wedding, June 2, 1959.

Che and Aleida's wedding, June 2, 1959.

Che and Aleida's wedding, June 2, 1959.

A trip to Bayamo.

Farewell at the airport when Che left on a trip to visit the Bandung Pact (nonaligned) countries, June 12, 1959.

Departure of the Cuban delegation to the Latin American Women's Congress in Chile. Aleida was a member of that delegation.

Departure of the Cuban delegation to the Latin American Women's Congress in Chile.

Che and Aleida at a political rally on January 28, 1960.

Aleida with Vilma Espín in Lima, Peru, on their return from the Latin American Women's Congress in Chile.

Aleida and Che at a political rally, January 1960.

At the Bellas Artes gallery, 1960.

At an event of the Federation of Cuban Women with Lidia Castro, Calixta Guiteras and Che's mother Celia de la Serna (right).

Photo taken by Che.

On the way to Baracoa on the Toa River.

Postcard to Aleida sent by Che from Shanghai.

Ciudad Libertad, Havana, with a German delegation, 1960.

With Aleidita (their first child) in their home in Miramar (1961).

Voluntary work with a Chinese delegation.

Aleida during a 1961 trip to China, as head of a delegation of the Federation of Cuban Women.

During the 1961 Federation of Cuban Women's trip to China.

During the 1961 Federation of Cuban Women's trip to China.

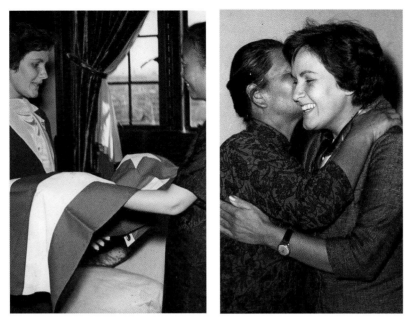

During the 1961 Federation of Cuban Women's trip to China.

During the 1961 Federation of Cuban Women's trip to China.

Meeting Che at the airport on his return from one of his trips to the Soviet Union.

Our household included Téllez, del Sol, Díaz the cook, and also Castillo, all of whom had come with us from La Cabaña. Some of these compañeros made up part of the permanent security garrison in our various houses over the next few years. Che implemented a disciplined regime for the men, including formal lessons with a teacher so that the soldiers of Che's bodyguard could maintain their education program.

Che and I had a few misunderstandings. Once a group of Nicaraguans came to the house and, to my surprise, Che sent me out of the room while they met. I didn't understand this because I had attended similar meetings with the Dominicans, Panamanians and Haitians. I left the room and started to cry, beginning to doubt whether Che trusted me. He explained later that he had expected it to be a very tense meeting, when unpleasant things would be said that he didn't want me to hear. He apologized, saying he had expected the Nicaraguans to be quite agitated. I came to understand the importance of these meetings.

If I regret anything now, it would be my failure to understand the need to document such meetings for posterity, even by taking brief notes. None of us really understood the extent or real significance of what was happening, nor the transcendent nature of our role in the development of groups that came to lead liberation movements throughout Latin America. I wasn't asked to take notes of those meetings, even though I was always present. Now, when I want to write about those events, I can't remember everything because of the years that have passed.

One of the revolutionary laws most eagerly anticipated in Cuba—the Agrarian Reform Law—was drafted in that house in the little seaside town of Tarará. Che assumed this responsibility, mainly because Fidel had given him and Sorí Marín that task during the Sierra Maestra days. On reaching the Escambray Mountains, Che applied the law promulgated in the Sierra

Maestra in the new territories under his command. The drafting meetings took place on a daily basis over many nights. Fidel was living nearby in Cojímar at the time and he came as often as he could. Others attending these meetings were Raúl and Vilma, Núñez Jiménez, Oscar Pino Santos and Alfredo Guevara. The final draft of the document was presented in May 1959.

Carlos Rafael Rodríguez* would also visit our house regularly, and I remember his visits well. They would stay up practically the entire night discussing revolutionary theory and practice. These discussions preceded a debate on political economy and the transition to a post-capitalist society, a debate in which both Che and Carlos Rafael were key participants.**

Not everything went entirely smoothly in Tarará. There was a misunderstanding about my first pregnancy and miscarriage. I had gone to an event at the Capitolio, where I had a fall. That night I started to bleed and, as a result, I had to have an abortion the next day. I went to the hospital with Fernández Mell because Che, being such a well-known figure, felt he couldn't take me, and he wanted to avoid the attention. Che was very upset about what had happened. He thought I had wanted an abortion because we weren't yet married. I could not convince him that was not the case. I was not able to get pregnant again for another eight months, and he often joked that he, like the Shah of Iran, could not have children.

By the end of April, there was great excitement throughout the island. For the first time in Cuban history, we would have a May Day celebration that was a true expression of the Cuban workers' power. Che had recovered from his illness, so we were

---

* Carlos Rafael Rodríguez was a leader of the Popular Socialist Party (PSP).

** See Ernesto Che Guevara et al: *The Great Debate on Political Economy and Revolution* (Ocean Press, 2012).

able to travel to Santiago de Cuba for the celebration in the company of Calixto García, Manuel Piñeiro and compañeros of the Revolutionary Directorate. I can still see the people marching with joy, for the first time in their lives envisaging a better future. The weapons carried by the soldiers were no longer used to repress the Cuban people. Instead the rebel soldiers were mixed in with the masses who carried tools to be used in the construction of a new society. It was the exuberant expression of a united people, willing to defend what they had won.

On May 3 we traveled to Las Villas province, passing through Sancti Spiritus, where we met up with Camilo. That was where Che exchanged his beret for Camilo's hat, an incident captured in a famous photograph. In Santa Clara, we met my family, whom I had not seen for some months. I stayed with them for a few days and then returned to Havana alone. A few weeks later, on May 29, Che came to tell me Hilda had finally signed the divorce papers. We could then commence the preparations for our wedding. He also officially informed my parents. We then moved to a new home, a rented farm house near Santiago de las Vegas, a pleasant location, slightly outside the city.

I returned to Santa Clara so that a friend could make my wedding dress, a very simple dress. I would often stay at Lolita's house when I traveled to Santa Clara so that my parent's traditional attitude was not challenged. The wedding took place on June 2, 1959, at La Cabaña Fortress. We wanted an informal ceremony, and Hilda had requested that no media attend the wedding. But when Raúl Castro found out, he took it upon himself to organize a party for us. I got dressed at Lupe's home, and the marriage ceremony took place at Alberto Castellanos's home in the fortress. Everything was modest, with only a few people officially invited. We thought there would be no celebration or toast, and only a small group of people. But others conspired against this and organized a big party, attended by Raúl and his wife Vilma, Celia Sánchez and her sisters, my family and some friends from Santa Clara, as well as compañeros from Che's column. Later on Camilo and Efigenio Ameijeiras (who was chief of police and who, incidentally, got a speeding ticket that night), arrived bringing others I didn't really know. Everyone signed the guest book. Unfortunately, nobody had told Fidel, the celebration having been organized in semi-clandestine manner. He showed up complaining he hadn't been invited. He signed the guest book, and then he left shortly afterwards. That is how our wedding took place. The next day it was front page news.

The wedding was a natural step in our relationship, the culmination of the first stage in our life together—a brief, intense and extremely happy period. After the party, we returned to our home in Santiago de las Vegas for our honeymoon. Juan Almeida was waiting at the house to congratulate us, so we chatted with him for a while. Then, finally, we had time to ourselves. But it was very brief as early the next morning Che's daughter, Hildita, arrived. Her mother had sent her as a wedding gift, maybe thinking we wouldn't want to have Hildita living with us. But Che was always very happy to have his daughter with him. I remember he took some photos of Hildita, one with a cat we had at the time. This was the beginning of our married life.

We had some special moments at the Tarará house, and we also experienced wonderful times in our home in Santiago de las Vegas. The revolution was advancing at lightning speed. We were getting better organized and uniting all the revolutionary forces. Raúl Castro and Che held regular meetings with members of the Popular Socialist Party (the former communist party). These meetings were held in secret. They discussed how to overcome the anticommunist sentiment still very much alive in Cuba at the time. I have to admit I was still influenced by my rural background, and I told Che I didn't trust Aníbal Escalante* and some of the others who came to our house. It seemed like a conspiracy within another larger conspiracy.

I also met the Argentine Jorge Ricardo Masetti,** who was encouraged by Che to form the news agency Prensa Latina. Che originally proposed that I become the head of the press agency. He said he would help me with the experience he had gained in Mexico and the Sierra Maestra. But I refused, thinking I was not ready for the role. Perhaps that is why I always admired Haydee Santamaría, who demonstrated not only intelligence but also a fine sensibility when she became head of the prestigious cultural institution, Casa de las Américas, despite her lack of formal education.

During those months of hectic activity, I somehow managed to focus on my personal life: I finally learned to drive properly, I exercised and read a lot. I started to read Russian and Soviet literature, and my political views slowly began to "redden" under Che's influence — he always had great powers of persuasion. The more I came to know him, the more I understood his total dedication. He tried to convince me about communism, patiently clearing up my misconceptions, without me feeling that he was forcing his views on me. We talked about all kinds of things, including some of the issues that arose during the revolutionary war such as the relative importance of the urban underground movement and the guerrilla struggle in the mountains.***

---

* The main revolutionary forces that had opposed the Batista dictatorship were the July 26 Movement, the Revolutionary Directorate and the Popular Socialist Party (PSP). These three organizations fused into the Integrated Revolutionary Organizations (ORI) in 1961. Aníbal Escalante, formerly the organization secretary of the PSP, later played a destructive role in the new party.

** Jorge Ricardo Masetti, an Argentine journalist, was the founder and director of Prensa Latina news agency. He was killed in combat in a guerrilla action in Salta, northern Argentina, in April 1964.

*** This debate is often referred to as the *Sierra* (mountains) vs the *Llano* (plains).

Che had many responsibilities in the new revolutionary government. In May 1959, Fidel suggested Che travel to the countries comprising the Bandung Pact. This international alliance later formed the Movement of Nonaligned Countries. Fidel always placed great importance on our relationship with these countries, and their support for Cuba at the United Nations General Assembly was decisive. This also meant we dealt with representatives of those countries as equals. That trip led to Che becoming the principal representative of Cuba's foreign policy.

Nevertheless, the trip came at a difficult time for me. Che left Cuba on June 12 — only 10 days after our wedding — and he didn't return until September. Due to the length of time he would be away, I suggested I go along as his secretary. He strongly rejected this idea. This taught me a lot. He argued that, apart from being his secretary, I was also his wife, and it would be seen as a privilege if I were to go on the trip with him, when other wives or girlfriends were not able to. Before he left, we went to see Fidel, and he also tried to convince Che to take me along. But Che would not be moved. I started to cry, and this made him angry. It was a difficult time for him, too, and I was making it worse. While Che was away on that extended trip, Fidel suggested I join him in Morocco or Japan; but Che would still not change his mind. Instead, he sent me postcards from those faraway, exotic places, describing his experiences. The first one arrived from Japan:

My darling,

Today I write to you from Hiroshima, where the bomb was dropped. On the catafalque that you can see are the names of more than 78,000 people who died, the total number is estimated to be 180,000.

It is good to visit this place so that we can fight for peace with more energy.

Big hug,

Che

Towards the end of the trip he wrote from Morocco, this time in a lighter tone, expressing his eagerness to return home:

Aleiducha,

From the last leg of the journey I send you a faithful marital hug. I had hoped to remain faithful, even with my thoughts. But the local Moorish women here are truly stunning...

Kisses,

Che

Perhaps because he felt slightly guilty about this trip, Che always spoke about us taking a trip together to Mexico, so that I could see for myself that country and its wonderful Mayan and Aztec cultures. This was, of course, just a fantasy because we faced such a huge workload. Nevertheless, the idea of traveling together remained our fantasy.

On his return from that first major overseas trip, Che quickly resumed his incredible workload. On August 7, 1959, he was designated head of the Department of Industry of the National Institute of Agrarian Reform (INRA). He asked me to come and work for him as his personal secretary. I was reluctant at first, but when he told me, with an ironic grin, he had been assigned a pretty secretary, I changed my mind. I reported for work at his office the very next morning.

My future role had been decided in the first days of January when, on a trip around Havana, Raúl Castro asked Che what rank I would be honored with. Che bluntly replied, none, because I would be his wife. I accepted this, although some may not understand my position. I have never regretted the decision, which I think brought us closer together and helped reinforce our relationship, especially for Che, who had been alone for such a long time.

We wanted to make a home with children. I didn't care about appearing in photos with famous celebrities. I was happy in my anonymity, always taking pleasure just in being by Che's side. Was this because I suspected we might not have much time together? I know how happy he was in those days, in the few moments in which he could escape into our private world. In a letter he wrote to me years later from Paris (in 1965) he commented: "I am definitely getting old. I am more in love with you each day and my home beckons me—the children and the little world that I can only sense rather than experience. Sometimes, I think this is dangerous, diverting me from my duty. Moreover, you are so essential to me and I am only a habit for you…"

When I went to Che's INRA office on that first day, despite what Che had told me, to my surprise I bumped into an extremely pretty girl, well-groomed according to the fashion of the time. I immediately asked who she was and what she was doing there. They explained she was the wife of Nuñez Jiménez (director of INRA) and he had assigned her to work as Che's secretary. I requested she leave immediately because I was the only secretary Che needed. Everyone else in the office agreed and covered up the fact that I was responsible for the removal of the director's wife.

When Che arrived, he made a sarcastic comment about his new secretary having disappeared, and he reminded me he was not the head of INRA. It wasn't until many years later, when we were in Tanzania, that I finally confessed my part in the secretary's disappearance. By that time I no longer experienced such bouts of jealousy, and he would actually complain I was no longer as jealous as I had been! He didn't realize that by then I was far more secure in our relationship.

Despite my reputation as a jealous wife, in my role as his personal secretary I never read Che's private letters; he knew this and trusted me completely. On one occasion, a compañero asked him why he had me as his secretary and why he would want to work with his wife. Che replied with good humor, and with no ill feeling, that the decision had been entirely his, and he was very happy to work with his wife.

The work piled up, especially after the revolutionary government's Law No. 851 (Article III) passed on June 6, 1959, giving INRA responsibility for the Department of Industry. This responsibility included the Cuban Institute of Oil and the administration of all expropriated companies.

At this stage the first plans for industrialization were made, the main objective being to create industries that would save precious dollars by producing a range of urgently needed consumer goods that could substitute for imports.

Che recognized the importance of nickel mining. Cuba has large reserves of this metal, and processing plants had been built and exploited by US companies in Oriente province. In order to operate the plants, we needed special technology that the Yankees refused to share with us after the plants were expropriated.

Cuba not only needed skilled technicians, but also needed people to put their hearts and souls into meeting the challenge of industrialization, qualities Che had in abundance. He was greatly assisted by Demetrio Presilla, an engineer and the only technician who had stayed working at the Moa mine after the revolution.

Given the importance of the mining industry, we traveled almost every weekend to that area in the far east of the island. The plant was eventually reopened and contributed significantly to the economic development of our country.

Che made a point of meeting some of the nickel miners to learn first hand about their appalling exploitation. They had a poor diet and little education. Their grueling physical labor, and its contribution to the economy, was not recognized. Gradually measures were taken to humanize their work, and the miners gained a sense of dignity. They were immediately provided with better food in workers' meal rooms and they were allocated better housing. For the first time in their lives they were treated like human beings. Che took a great interest in these previously neglected mining communities. He even took photos of one place called Imías.

José Manuel Manresa worked at INRA's Department of Industry as office manager, and *El Patojo* (Che's Guatemalan friend) acted as his assistant. Other Latin Americans also collaborated with the department, including economists Juan Noyola, Carlos Romeo, Jaime Barrios, Álvaro Latoste, Raúl Maldonado and others, all of whom followed Che when he went to work at the National Bank. Most of them were advisers in the project that eventually became the Ministry of Industry. They also carried out tasks related to the nationalization of factories, the collection of taxes, assisting with queries and complaints, and dealing with large companies such as the sugar mills and tobacco manufacturers like Partagas.

Aside from reopening the key mining complex at Moa, in the first year of the revolution Che was also involved in the construction of the "Camilo Cienfuegos" school complex in El Caney de las Mercedes. This work was carried out by Che's former column. In the months of June and July, part of the column was sent to Oriente and another part went to Santa Clara.

The construction of the school complex fulfilled one of Che's dreams. He thoroughly enjoyed his visits there, laboring alongside his compañeros.

When Che was named president of the National Bank on November 29, 1959, we moved house again, this time to Ciudad Libertad, formerly Batista's military camp (Camp Columbia), which was later transformed into a large school campus. Raúl Castro and his wife, Vilma, and other compañeros also lived in Ciudad Libertad at the time.

In the whirlwind of the first year of the revolution, Che played a part in the formation of the G-2 Cuban Intelligence Service, formed to guarantee the safety of the revolution. He was also in charge of the first delegations arriving from socialist countries, without ever neglecting his other multiple responsibilities.

Sometimes Che had to resolve minor problems involving the members of his bodyguard, for example when his compañero Harry Villegas accidentally fired a shot killing another compañero when the bullet ricocheted off a wall. Che sent Villegas to La Cabaña to be detained and serve his sentence. This showed that, for Che, discipline came first, with no exemptions for anyone.

Che's work at the National Bank was very stressful, because it meant creating an entirely new kind of bank. This required a massive effort and substantial time. Che immediately proposed new measures to stop the flight of capital from the country, which included breaking ties with the International Monetary Fund to which Cuba belonged and was meant to contribute $25 million. The Economic and Social Development Bank was liquidated along with the National Finance Company and the Cuban Foreign Commerce Bank, institutions that represented a drain on national funds.

An official of Cuba's National Bank was ordered to withdraw Cuba's gold deposits held in the United States. US banks in Cuba, including the Chase Manhattan Bank, the First National Bank of

Boston and Citibank of New York, were all nationalized. A law was later passed nationalizing all Cuban and foreign banks, with the exception of Canadian banks. Another 44 banking enterprises were also nationalized along with their 325 offices and branches at 96 locations throughout the country. We purchased the two remaining Canadian banks, and a successful currency exchange occurred in 1961. This became possible when the first contracts were signed with the socialist countries in 1960. The famous bank notes with the simple signature "Che" were printed in Czechoslovakia.

All of this activity emanated from the central office of the National Bank with its tiny staff that included José Manuel Manresa, a highly qualified bilingual secretary named Luisa (whose surname I forget) and me as personal secretary, along with a group of assistants. Some changes had to be made because the carpet in Che's office aggravated his asthma. It was replaced with a linoleum floor. We enjoyed our time there, despite the enormous workload. We felt like a little family, eating breakfast and lunch together at the far end of the building, near Che's office. We had no fixed routine: we might eat at 8:00 p.m. or 3:00 in the morning, when we would have a hot chocolate with toast. We always enjoyed the company of other Latin Americans, who would tell anecdotes about their countries. This helped us to get to know one another better. Among these visitors were Carlos Romeo, Jaime Barrios, Raúl Maldonado, José Santiestaben and Salvador Vilaseca, a Cuban who later became Che's mathematics tutor and who remained with him until Che transferred to the Ministry of Industry.

Among our memorable visitors was the Soviet delegation led by Eugenio Kosarev, a loyal supporter of Cuba, who became one of Che's close friends. Somehow a typewriter with Russian characters materialized so that he could type up his reports. It might have been Graciela Rivas who found that typewriter—she was incredibly efficient. She was Manuel Aspuru San Pedro's attorney and always did her best to assist us.

Another of our regular visitors was Jaime Barrios, a Chilean collaborator, who later died alongside President Salvador Allende at La Moneda Palace, during the tragic events surrounding the military coup on September 11, 1973.

At this time Che began to attend the official government receptions, something he didn't particularly relish. He also attended the new cadre school and he would get very annoyed if a compañero failed to attend classes. Wherever he went, Che always wore his olive green uniform, which by evening would look quite crumpled and sometimes even dirty, depending on what he had been doing that day.

I remember one particular reception when Regino Boti, our finance minister and a good friend of Che's with a great sense of humor, urgently called me over to tell me something. He commented, in a low voice, on how elegant Che looked that night. I glanced over at Che whose boots looked scuffed, as they always did, and whose uniform looked the same, a little crumpled perhaps. I couldn't discern anything unusual in his attire, so I asked Regino what he meant. "Look," he said, "he has not one, not two, but three pens in his pocket!"

Often, when we were ready to leave work and go home in the early hours of the morning, Alberto Bayo would show up to play chess with Che. Che had so little leisure time and so few pastimes that I would let them be. But this usually meant we would leave the bank almost as the sun was rising and we would be in a bad mood the next day.

Che always made time in his busy schedule to follow the construction of the "Camilo Cienfuegos" school complex. We would go there every week, always with Eliseo, a skilled pilot but, nevertheless, not immune from accidents. One day we got caught in a storm that nearly brought the light aircraft down. After Camilo* died in a plane crash, we were prohibited from flying in these little planes, and we had to travel in a Cessna with two motors.

For Che these trips in light aircraft had many purposes; he loved to fly and usually piloted the plane himself. Sometimes he would fly over central Cuba along the route from the Sierra Maestra to Santa Clara, recapturing his experiences during the revolutionary war. When we reached our destination, Che would be in a great mood, taking charge of everything, chatting to the soldiers of his former column and asking about everything in great detail. We stayed the night sometimes, sleeping in bunk beds; he would take the top bunk and bring his hand down to hold mine— we would fall asleep that way. Despite the fact we were working, these were most enjoyable trips.

On one of our last visits to the school, we met Sidroc Ramos, who had just been named as its director. His wife, Berarda Salabarría, also worked at the school. The children were yet to arrive. Then in the distance, we saw them coming toward us, led by Isabel Rielo, who had been the captain of the all-female "Mariana Grajales" squad in the Sierra Maestra. I found it very moving, recalling my own painful separation from my family when I had to go to Santa Clara to study. If I had any talent for painting, I would like to have painted that beautiful scene. The children came from some of the most remote parts of the island, and would never have had a chance to study without this school. Their parents were happy for their children to be educated and showed confidence in the revolution. I remember how those children saw electric lights for the first time, commenting with

---

* Camilo Cienfuegos (1932-1959) was a *Granma* expeditionary. As commander of the Second Column "Antonio Maceo" he led the Rebel Army's invasion of the northern region of Las Villas, central Cuba. After the revolution, he became head of the Rebel Army, but died in an airplane accident on October 28, 1959.

surprise that the stars seemed very low in the sky that night. Such experiences filled us all, especially Che, with a great sense of satisfaction.

In November 1959, as part of a large Cuban delegation of more than 80 women compañeras from all social spheres, I attended the Latin American Congress of Women held in Chile. The Federation of Cuban Women (FMC) and other mass organizations did not yet exist. Nevertheless, prior to the congress we worked in commissions on different themes, with the aim of explaining to others the work of our fledgling revolution.

Che came to see us off at the airport, convinced about the significance of this trip for Cuba and for all of us. This was my first trip abroad. He was not mistaken about the importance of the tour. Journalists followed our every move in Chile, asking us about what was happening in Cuba. I appeared on the front page of one paper as "Mrs. Guevara." It was a real learning experience for us, as we met labor movement leaders from many different countries. We confidently and effectively explained Cuba's revolutionary process to anyone who would listen.

Chileans approached us in the street, questioning us about the changes that were taking place in Cuba. We met Salvador Allende (then a member of parliament) and dined at his house, along with the leaders of other delegations. This gave me my first glimpse into the world of diplomacy. I have but one regret about that trip: that I didn't get to meet Pablo Neruda, one of Che's favorite poets.

We returned to Cuba via Lima, where we took advantage of the opportunity to see some of the city's magnificent old colonial buildings with their beautiful balconies. We were anxious to get home, to relate our experiences and especially to be reunited with our partners. Most of us did not want long separations at that time.

The year came to an end, bringing a feeling of satisfaction about what we had accomplished and about the revolution itself. On December 31 we went to the home of our friends Armando Hart and Haydee Santamaría to celebrate New Year's Eve. Spirits were extremely high that night. Haydee announced she would celebrate her birthday on that date from then on. That night Che danced with Adita, Haydee's younger sister. To be honest, although he might have wanted to dance, he was a dreadful dancer. He danced in a clownish manner, radiating the joy we all felt. We went home at six in the morning.

The year 1959 had certainly brought about profound changes in our lives. With Che, I felt I was experiencing the best moments of my life—maybe not in the way my romantic novels ended, but I never doubted I belonged with him. Besides, every day I admired him more for his devotion, loyalty and integrity. The more time we spent together, the stronger was the attachment between us.

In a romantic mood, he sent me a postcard from Egypt in 1965, during the last of his extended trips overseas:

> *Madam,*
>
> *Through these two doors, solitude escaped and went in search of your green island.*
>
> *I don't know if one day we'll be able to hold hands, surrounded by children, admiring the view from some vestige of the past; if that's not possible, let it be your dream.*
>
> *I respectfully kiss your hand,*
>
> > *Your little husband*

7

That first year of the revolution soon made me and many others realize the limits of our education. This was, of course, compensated for by our tremendous desire to overcome all obstacles, breaking with the old ways. But it wasn't easy. On a personal level, Che helped me a great deal. He was a brilliant teacher, leading me by his daily example. But some things I had to figure out for myself, like how to juggle my roles as a wife, mother and worker.

The year 1960 opened with the wonderful, exciting news of another pregnancy. In the first few months I needed special attention from Dr. Celestino Alvarez Lajonchere, who became my gynecologist and subsequently delivered all our children. I also relied on the support of our doctor, Fernández Mell, an old friend and compañero. Celia Sánchez was also extremely helpful in those first few months, as was Che's mother, who was staying with us at the time. I was supposed to rest; but when my father had a heart attack, I desperately wanted to go to Santa Clara to see him. Che was in the middle of a very important meeting when he heard the news. Concerned about me, he asked Eliseo to take me to Santa Clara by plane.

Che joined us most unexpectedly the next day. I was sitting beside my father as he lay in bed, tending to him as only a daughter can, when I was startled by a voice behind me. Che had dropped everything to be there with me. When we were confident my father was going to recover, we returned to Havana together.

Around this time it was decided to transform the former

military Camp Columbia (Ciudad Libertad) into a massive school complex. Most of us who had been living there now had to move. Che and I moved to another home on 18th Street, near 7th and 9th, in Miramar, Havana. We only stayed there relatively briefly from April 1960 to October of 1962, but because of the events on both a personal and historic level that took place while we were living there, that house became very special to us.

During the Bay of Pigs invasion in April 1961, two airports in Havana (Ciudad Libertad and San Antonio de los Banos) were bombed, as was the airport in Santiago de Cuba. The October Missile Crisis occurred the following year (1962). In the midst of these crises, our first two children were born. Our daughter Aleidita arrived on November 24, 1960, and Camilo, the long-awaited son, on May 20, 1962. Che was head of the National Bank and the Department of Industry at INRA, but after all industries were nationalized in August 1960, he assumed responsibility for what became the Ministry of Industry. His political activities intensified, both on a national and international level.

In October 1960, Che led a delegation to China to sign the first trade agreements with a socialist country. Before he left, we discussed names for our first child. Che was convinced the baby was a boy. He wanted to break with tradition and not name his first son Ernesto. So we agreed that the boy would be named Camilo after his dearest friend and comrade-in-arms, Camilo Cienfuegos, who had died the previous year.

We never anticipated the birth of a girl. With his usual dry wit, Che sent me a cheerful telegram from China saying that if, by some chance, the baby was a girl, she should be thrown over the balcony. The baby wasn't named until Che returned from his trip because neither of us had considered girls' names.

He was in Shanghai when he heard the news. He sent me a postcard:

In this city I found out about our new acquisition.

You are always making sure that I come out looking bad.

Well, anyway, I send you both a kiss, and remember, don't cry over spilled milk.

Hugs,

Che

He returned with a beautiful quilt as a gift for the baby, whom he said should be called Aleida. He considered it an unusual name and thought it had a musical ring to it. I didn't want to challenge him on this, given that I knew he had no ear at all for music. But I appreciated him saying he had always liked the name Aleida after he heard it on the radio before he met me. The Aleida mentioned on the radio was a revolutionary combatant, Aleida Fernández Chardié, killed by the Batista dictatorship.

Che returned from China with a good picture of what was happening in other socialist countries, and he started to question some of the differences that existed between them. He was particularly interested in different approaches to achieving the transition to socialism. He was very enthusiastic about what he had seen in China. He admired the way they worked and how they were meeting the challenge of development. He was acutely aware that China, in only 11 years, had emerged from terrible famine. He was impressed by their approach to work and their dedication to the construction of socialism. He often remarked that China was like a living museum of humanity, where you could see the most ancient work tools and the most modern ones, all used with great efficiency.

His enthusiasm for what he had seen in China earned Che the reputation of being a Maoist and pro-China. But his primary

interest was evaluating what lessons could be applied to Cuba
in its path to socialism. In contrast to his positive impression
of China, Che was critical of what he saw in the Soviet Union,
especially the privileges some leaders enjoyed. Nevertheless, he
recognized the spirit of the people and of their revolution. This is
how he described it to me in a letter:

> *My darling,*
>
> *I take a few moments in my hectic tour of Stalingrad to
> send you this postcard.*
>
> *Here one truly encounters one of the greatest epics in
> history.*
>
> *I will be in China in two days.*
>
> *Kisses,*
>
> *Che*

He made similar comments about Prague, a city of infinite beauty.
He was struck by the splendor of its architecture, but he also
remarked the hotels were full of women who appeared to be
prostitutes or members of the old class system. Che had always
abhorred prostitution.

As the year ended, on New Year's Eve Fidel and Che discussed
many plans and projects at our home. They didn't regularly have
the chance for a relaxed chat, but the empathy and affection
between the two men was striking to any observer.

The Federation of Cuban Women (FMC) was organized
in 1960. Led by Vilma Espín, it played a very important role in
involving women in the tasks and challenges of the revolution. Its
goal was the full integration of women into society, eliminating

all barriers and restrictions. This was by no means an easy fight because we had to confront persistent male chauvinism that often blocked the incorporation of women into activities outside the home. Moreover, many Cuban women were virtually illiterate or had a very low cultural level.

We saw none of this as insurmountable. We were most proud of our achievements in improving the lives of former maids and prostitutes; we felt this said a lot about the objectives of our organization. I was part of the national executive of the FMC from its inception until the end of 1964, when our son Ernesto was born. My first role was as national treasurer since I had efficiently managed the funds during our trip to Chile in November 1959. We all worked incredibly hard during those first years and learned so much.

As the US government stepped up its support for the counter-revolutionary groups inside Cuba, we called on members of the FMC to join the National Revolutionary Militia. Women showed themselves ready to defend the country and everything we had gained with the revolution. I had to juggle housework, work and four children, who had been born almost within a year of each other. Without day care, care in primary schools and the scholarships and other important educational programs initiated by the revolutionary government, women like me would never have been able to do what we wanted to do.

The results of the FMC's work were clearly evident. The monthly membership fee helped establish regular and direct contact with every member at a grass roots level. In this way, we formed a movement of cadres on a national level; I was a professional cadre, although I was never paid for my work. The first congress of the FMC was held in 1962, where I was elected general secretary and Vilma Espín was elected president. I was able to fulfill my role as FMC general secretary without neglecting my other work as Che's personal secretary; I could always count on Vilma's support and her advice about how to carry out tasks more efficiently and with greater unity. She was particularly helpful to me during difficult times, such as during the internal party fight against sectarianism that was particularly sharp in my province.

Che had a boundless faith in Fidel and was one of his closest collaborators. He was profoundly affected by the way the Cuban people, not caring that he was Argentine, had adopted him as one of their own. This reinforced the Latin Americanism he had embraced as a young medical student on his first travels around the continent.

In Mexico, before arriving in Cuba with the guerrilla expedition, Che had written a poem called "Song for Fidel," in which he already identified himself as a Cuban.

It begins,

> *Onward,*
> *burning prophet of the dawn,*
> *down hidden and untouched paths,*
> *to liberate the green* caimán* *you love so well.*

The last verse begins:

> *And if our path is blocked by iron,*
> *we ask only a rosary of Cuban tears...*

Even when he was most infuriated by something in Cuba, he would always refer to "we Cubans," never feeling that he didn't belong, even though he hadn't been born in our country.

The Ministry of Industry was formed on February 23, 1961, and

---

* Alligator: a reference to the island of Cuba, whose shape resembles that animal.

Che was appointed minister. Much has been written about Che's work in this role—both favorable and critical. I don't doubt that he made mistakes and that there were problems others would have experienced. But he did his best in applying all his skill to this role with a passion and commitment to something he saw as essential for the development and advancement of the revolution.

The Ministry of Industry was structured in such a way as to leave no room for schemas or rigidity but to be able to respond to the greatest challenge of the revolution—industrialization. It represented a stage beyond the first experimental phase in the Sierra Maestra, where Che organized small factories to make simple products to meet the needs of the guerrillas' camps. When Che first arrived at La Cabaña, he immediately organized small local workshops to satisfy the demands of the troops. All this was in accord with the objectives of the revolutionary program Fidel had outlined in 1953.

With this previous experience and a skilled team around him, Che proposed the reactivation of the industrial sector in our country. In particular, this meant ending the sugar monoculture as the way to break out of Cuba's neocolonial status and underdevelopment. This was a gigantic challenge that only someone like Che could have undertaken, given his willingness to work, his sense of responsibility, his creative spirit, as well as his ability to study and reflect on what he was doing.

In creating the new ministry, there were hundreds of hours of discussions, and Che was always at the center of these debates. The work also involved establishing vice-ministries, directors and branches in the restructure of nationalized businesses and factories. Eventually an integrated system of organization, direction and planning in all industrial activity was created.

Many Latin American consultants assisted in this, a number of whom had already worked with Che on other projects. Some of them belonged to the Economic Commission for Latin America and the Caribbean (CEPALC)* and others were from the United Nations. Progressive intellectuals and economists from various socialist countries also participated.

In this way Cuba made initial steps toward industrialization. New branches of industry such as automation and electronics were established, as well as research centers. Che's passion and signature were evident in all these achievements that represented, as he put it, "the purest of our hopes." In this, he was contributing in a practical way to what he referred to as "the new man."

Meanwhile, Che also played a role in the foreign policy of the revolutionary government, through which we became familiar with other countries' efforts to create a socialist system. Specialists came from other socialist countries to assist in the creation of the Ministry of Industry, bringing the scientific and technical expertise Cuba badly needed. Being intimately involved in Che's work as his secretary with this challenge, I saw how Che grew and learned from the process.

By 1961, the revolution was advancing and the decades of corruption and pillage were coming to an end, as the Cuban people began to shape their own future. Cuba's enemies felt their most treasured possession slipping from their grasp, and the counterrevolutionary forces prepared to launch a full-scale assault.

Che was assigned as the chief military officer for the western region of the island. When the first attack occurred in April 1961, Che left immediately for Pinar del Río. The entire population was mobilized; I was part of the FMC's effort.

---

* The Economic Commission for Latin America and the Caribbean was one of the five UN regional commissions created on February 28, 1948, by the Economic and Social Council and the Economic Commission for Latin America (CEPAL).

When I learned Che had been injured, I wanted to go to Pinar del Río immediately to see him. He had asked that I not be told of what had happened, or at least not until the seriousness of his injury was established. But it was impossible to contain the news and, in fact, it was Fidel who told me—he was always understanding and a true friend. I took our daughter Aliucha (that's what we called Aleidita) to Celia Sánchez's house at her suggestion, because it was considered to be a safe place. Not knowing in what state I would find Che, I set out on a very anxious trip. There were tanks and mobilized combatants all along the highway, preparing for the invasion.

I arrived at dawn to find Che recovering from an operation. I approached him nervously, but I could see he was OK. When I remarked I was happy his injury wasn't more serious and that the bullet had not damaged a vital organ, he responded in a joking tone, "Damn luck! Of all the bullets this one had to land on me!" Then he went on to explain what had happened. In a moment of carelessness he had dropped his gun without properly securing it. The bullet hit him in the cheek and exited from behind his ear; if it had been just a few millimeters off course the result would have been very different.

When the Bay of Pigs invasion began on April 17, 1961, Che was still recovering. But the next day, against my advice, he went to meet with Fidel very near where the counterrevolutionaries had landed. It was thought there might be further attacks at Bahía Honda and Cabañas, areas under Che's command.

Che took me back to Havana at the same breakneck speed that I had traveled to see him. We picked up Aleidita from Celia's house, and he dropped us back home. I assumed Che would not be able to fight due to his injury. But I was mistaken. After discussing tactics with Fidel, he returned to Pinar del Río. He was there when we learned of the crushing defeat of the enemy. The other attacks did not occur; this had merely been an enemy ploy.

Our daily life resumed and we were more optimistic than before. The gigantic effort of the nationwide literacy campaign continued, reaching the most remote and neglected parts of the island. The literacy campaign was seen as an essential step to making a qualitative leap forward, not only guaranteeing the unconditional support of the masses for the revolution but also fully integrating them into the process and raising the cultural level of the entire country. The workers of the ministry participated in the literacy campaign by teaching classes in poor neighborhoods around Havana.

I taught in the then infamous (and quite dangerous) neighborhood of Las Yaguas. The family I was assigned to teach had suffered many traumas. The mother was only 39 years old but looked as though she was 60. She had a number of children, all from different fathers; they were all illiterate. I was able to teach one of the daughters, who was 14 or 15 years old. I taught her the first few letters of the alphabet with great effort. She was a maid in two houses, where she was only paid two and half pesos per month. Another daughter lived next door; I was not able to teach her. She was married to an alcoholic, and it was virtually impossible for me to even get close to her, as he wouldn't let me in the door. At the end of the campaign, through the FMC, I sought help for this family. We were able to convince the mother and one of the daughters to work. They went to Ciudad Libertad as part of the special scheme that offered scholarships to maids who had taken part in the literacy campaign so they could continue with their studies. They did learn to read and write, but we were not able to remove them entirely from their environment. That was a greater challenge.

Che backed me up in everything I did, both on a personal level and in family matters. My own family, too, needed help. We became guardians of my niece, Miriam, one of the daughters of my elder sister, who had died when I was a teenager. We contributed to her political and cultural development, and she became part of our family. When Miriam got married in 1965, the wedding was held in March, to fit in with Che's schedule. He wanted to be there so they waited until he came back from his trip through Africa. He lent the newlyweds his car for their honeymoon.

If I wanted to spend time with Che and carry out my own responsibilities, sometimes I had to leave the care of my children to others and abandon my role as a mother. I was supported in this by my family and the compañeros who lived nearby. Within the ministry, Manresa, who had been the office manager, and I agreed on a division of labor; I took charge of the personal correspondence.

I accompanied Che on the monthly visits he made to the provinces to check on the advances in the industrial sectors of the country. He always wanted to get as close as possible to the workers, in order to get a real sense of their needs as well as being able to contribute to finding solutions to problems. I would use my skills as a secretary to take notes of discussions and share some of the workload. We would enjoy these times together, being able to share an intimacy that we could not have had under other circumstances. Eventually I was able to come to terms with my feelings of jealousy. I came to understand that Che took his work very seriously and did not allow minor distractions to get in the way.

Over time, these visits to the provinces became more frequent and stressful. He wanted to be constantly informed about what was happening and was always alert to complacent or bureaucratic attitudes to administration, which he saw as the greatest danger of other socialist systems. He often referred to the party, the administrative apparatus and the labor movement as the "Holy Trinity." In his writings, he constantly warned of the serious problems created when the party, especially in the provinces, substituted itself for the administrative apparatus.

He visited important developments in other places such as the southern coast of Santiago de Cuba or El Caney de las Mercedes. If he thought there were problems, he would make a note and pass on the information to the relevant ministry.

He would contact the *campesinos* in those areas, listening to their problems. There were some interesting cases, like that of Argelio Rosabal, a Baptist from Sierra Maestra. He had approached Che and his group just after they disembarked from the *Granma*. Argelio later asked for some land on which to build a church, and this was granted at the beginning of 1959. Later on, someone tried to take this land away from him. Che took steps to have the land returned to Argelio. There was also Polo Torres, the "barefoot captain," who had seen a lot of action in Che's column. Whenever Che visited the area, he would seek him out to discuss what was happening locally.

Somehow we built our intimate space around Che's enormous workload and the odd hours that he kept. He would get up at 9:00 or 10:00 in the morning, drink some bitter coffee and gulp down some milk pudding, one of his favorite foods. He would sit at the table in the kitchen while I finished preparing his breakfast. While I made his coffee, he would drink carbonated water from a green glass that he liked to use. He had a special coffee cup that I had given him. When he had to meet a visiting delegation arriving early at the airport or attend a meeting in the early hours of the morning, he would let me know that he would be staying at the ministry so that he could grab a couple of hours sleep; but that did not happen very often.

I usually left the house after 11:00 in the morning and would return at around 10:00 p.m. or even midnight, depending on the amount of work to be done. On a few occasions, we went to the cinema, the drive-in or the theatre. There was a little room at the Cuban Institute of Art and Cinematography (ICAIC) where we could watch movies. The director, Alfredo Guevara, was a highly cultured man and a close friend.

From the first, Che took part in the receptions at the various embassies as part of his role in foreign relations. Depending on my pregnancies, I would usually attend with him. He would call me from the office so that I could get ready, and we would meet at home or at the ministry, depending on how much time we had. There is one amusing story about my attendance at these receptions. Accidentally, on a crossed line, Che heard a comment about my clothes. He came home and asked me if it was true that I had worn the same dress seven times to these receptions. I corrected him, saying it wasn't seven but eight times. It was the only maternity dress that was more or less suitable for such occasions and I didn't want to show him up because he always wore his work clothes.

Some of our most enjoyable times together involved sharing books. Throughout his life he was a voracious reader, reading about a book a day, taking advantage of any spare moments he had traveling from one place to another. Among his favorite books were *Don Quixote*, which he had read more than six times, and Marx's *Capital*, which he considered a monument to human knowledge. He always encouraged me to read whatever he thought was important. We would then discuss those books. We read most of the important Latin American literary works, Russian stories and Soviet literature and the best US authors. Because I enjoyed reading historical novels, he suggested I study history. He also urged me to study economics in 1961. I didn't want to enroll at university at that point because Aliucha* was just a baby and I didn't want to spend so much time away from Che.

I have to confess, I didn't pay much attention to his negligent attitude to personal appearance. He loved a very hot bath to be prepared for him, almost like a ritual. He also liked his breakfast served to him — small things that I accepted about him, maybe because I foresaw what was to come — that our time together would be short.

Che made a return trip to the Soviet Union in 1961, to reinforce the ties between our two countries, while I traveled to China with an FMC delegation. I was pregnant with Camilo and I had to stop and rest a lot during my trip. I was very excited to visit China, perhaps because of what Che had told me about the country. I visited the communes, but I did not have the same reaction to China as Che. The Chinese had certainly achieved a great deal and it was truly astounding to see how socialism was being constructed in such a different way. But I was shocked to see the deprivation and restrictions, everyone dressed in identical uniforms.

Chinese people approached us and showed great warmth, expressing their admiration for Cuba and our revolution. We sang the July 26 Movement anthem together in Spanish; we were amazed at the efforts they made for us. It was quite an emotional experience in an immense country, so totally different from what we read in books and the international media.

In time I came to appreciate the enormous sacrifices the Chinese people had made in order to build a new country, especially when I better understood their long history and ancient culture. I went to the Soviet Union in November that same year, where I saw another level of socialist development. Before I left, I took a Russian language course and thought I had mastered some

---

* Aleidita was called Aliucha within the family.

of the vocabulary. But I was completely humiliated when I tried to speak Russian. Children would surround me every time I opened my mouth, and my compañeros from the delegation made no end of fun of me. Nevertheless, I enjoyed that trip.

Despite the years that have passed since the missile crisis of October (1962), I can still vividly recall the tension of the days when humanity faced an armed conflict of unimaginable proportions. After the Bay of Pigs, facing the constant threat of a US invasion, Cuba decided to accept the Soviet Union's offer to have nuclear missiles on our territory. We regarded this as a legitimate act in defense of our sovereignty.

The location of these strategic arms was detected by spy planes and denounced by the US government. Unfortunately, when the crisis came to a head, Cuba was not consulted and our revolutionary government was forced to take a principled stand, refusing to succumb to the threats of imperialism. The Soviet missiles were withdrawn, but we did not allow UN inspection.

In his farewell letter to Fidel, reflecting on the heroism demonstrated by the Cuban people at that time, Che wrote: "I have lived through magnificent days and, at your side, I felt the pride of belonging to our people during the brilliant yet sad days of the Caribbean [missile] crisis."*

In May 1962, there was another addition to our family. Che's greatest dream was fulfilled, his male ego finally boosted, with the birth of a son, Camilo. There are many anecdotes about what Che did when he heard the news of his son's arrival: that he smoked his cigar the wrong way, that he went to search for flowers for me but found none. Some of these stories are true, others aren't. But there was no doubt about the delight reflected in his face when he saw his son for the first time.

---

* Che's farewell letter to Fidel is included in *Che Guevara Reader* (Seven Stories Press, 2022).

The family was becoming quite large. We now had Hildita, Aliucha and Camilo, and two more children would arrive. We had the sense of creating our own little world, admittedly a rather unusual home, but nevertheless, an intimate refuge we shared with friends and family. We established the semblance of a routine that continued when we moved house yet again. But I had a sense of foreboding that this might be our last home together. And so it was.

The new house was in Nuevo Vedado, on 47th Street, between Conill and Tulipan. I chose it, Che agreeing rather reluctantly. I wanted a home separate from the garrison, somewhere I could be a bit more independent and not feel like I was always living in a barracks. We needed more time alone in our own home, when we weren't meeting our many commitments and responsibilities.

The security garrison moved next to the house, a short distance away. I now assumed the tasks of cooking, cleaning and other domestic duties, with the help of family and friends. Some members of the garrison, always regarded as part of the family, were a wonderful help. Rafael Hernández Calero (*Felo*) and Misael Fernández were pillars on whom I could lean, especially after Che's death. They were honest *campesinos*, a great comfort to the children, especially in the vacuum left by the absence of their father. Sofia Gato joined our household to help me with Aliucha, and she, too, became a member of the family. Of course, in mentioning members of our household, I can't leave out the famous Muralla, our loyal dog, about whom many legendary tales are told. He was given to me by a soldier in Che's column when we lived in Ciudad Libertad. He appears in many of the photos taken at that time.

Other lasting friends from those years are Harry Villegas, Alberto Castellanos, and Leonardo Tamayo. Another dear friend, Hermes Pena, a faithful compañero, was killed in Salta, Argentina, in the effort to extend the liberation of the Americas. There were others, like Carlos Coello (*Tuma*), who later went with Che on the missions to the Congo and Bolivia (where he was killed in combat); Felipe Hernández (*Chino*), also killed in Bolivia; and our doctor Oscar Fernández Mell lived with us before he got married.

I think the decision to move into our own home certainly brought us closer together, even though I never entirely liked that new house. From that time, we lived like the rest of the population, eating whatever food was available with the ration booklet that everyone had. I mention this in particular because I have read references to us having two ration booklets or a double ration. This misconception probably arose from something Che once said as a joke.

I managed our domestic affairs myself. I paid the rent, which was 40 pesos per month, out of Che's salary of 440 pesos. I did not receive a salary at the time. After Che left I received his salary; but as my children grew up and became independent, they gave up the benefit they received from the state. We generally lived according to the spirit of the revolution and Che's austere lifestyle.

Our next two children were born in the new house. Celia was born on June 14, 1963, hot on the heels of Camilo, then only 13 months old. Ernesto was born on February 24, 1965, when Che was in Algeria, on the last trip he made as a representative of the revolutionary government.

When he heard the news of the birth of his second son, he sent him a telegram, affectionately addressing the baby as "Tete," the pet name his family had given him when he was a little boy:

Ernesto Guevara March

(to be handed to him at his home or at the clinic)

Havana

Tete,

Tell the old woman I will not be home for dinner. Tell her to be good.

Give your brother and sisters a kiss.

Your old man

Algiers, 24-2-65

In spite of all these separations, our relationship became even stronger. I was in charge of the family and our home, and although they were not perfect, they were mine. I never worried too much about what we lacked. I knew we lived like every other Cuban who knew that sacrifices had to be made. I had a partner who perhaps on the surface did not attend to the details, but he would not stand for any privileges. Che never bothered much about material things, and that is how we lived. We never wanted for friends or family. We combined everyday tasks with the enjoyment of the small informal pleasures. We lived a simple life together, full of love, dreams and hopes.

We even enjoyed our voluntary workdays together. Che made no distinction between his regular, daily work and his extra voluntary labor. On learning of Che's death, Haydee Santamaria (an old friend and compañera) wrote a highly emotional letter addressed to Che, saying: "everything you created was perfect, but you made a unique creation, you made yourself, you showed how that new man was possible, we all saw how it could be a reality, because he exists, it was you."*

He participated in evening sessions of voluntary work in various companies over the years, managing to meet the required number of hours of voluntary labor almost magically. To this day, many people are astounded about how he managed to do so much voluntary work, given all the other responsibilities he had. He especially enjoyed working in the sugar cane harvests, where the entire population was mobilized.

Che was often the butt of jokes because of his defective musical ear. Once, at the end of a day of voluntary work, they played the national anthem and we all stood up. A little while later the July 26 Movement anthem was played. Che rose to his feet again, asking why the national anthem was being repeated. He was unable to distinguish between the two tunes.

On Sundays, after voluntary work and an arduous week at the ministry, Che would come home ready to enjoy the company of his children. He would take off his shirt and play with the children on the floor. We would then have lunch, always joined by a guest or two, and we would tell anecdotes around the table. Che would occasionally enjoy a glass of wine mixed with water — an Argentine custom he never lost; this was one of the few pleasures he enjoyed.

During his last period in Cuba, after lunch he would take a bath and then, in the afternoon, would go to the ministry for meetings with the heads of various companies. He was probably already planning for his departure, and he felt the need to leave everything organized. He was establishing his Budgetary Finance System** as an economic management system very different from

* See Betsy Maclean (ed.): *Haydee Santamaría* (Rebel Lives series, Ocean Press, 2003).

** "On the Budgetary Finance System" in *Che Guevara Reader* (Seven Stories Press, 2022).

how the economies in other socialist countries were run. Che rejected Marxism as a dogma, imbuing it with his own highly creative spirit.

Sometimes on Saturday nights, he liked to watch the boxing on television. Remembering this, I smile, because I could never understand how such a sensitive man enjoyed watching such a brutal sport. He would even pretend he was in the ring by throwing punches into the air while sitting in his chair. I never liked that sport—I hope all boxing fans will forgive me.

Che often worked in his office at home, which was on the more peaceful second floor. He enjoyed organizing that space, where he kept his most treasured books, most of them marked up with his notes or comments. This small room was his refuge. The books on the shelves reflected his wide range of interests, including universal literature and his favorite Latin American poets, like Pablo Neruda and César Vallejo. There are biographies, history, science, economy, general philosophy and, in particular, the classics of Marxist thought. There are also books on military strategy, essays on politics and sociology, chess handbooks and all kinds of other books. His notes in the books offer a fascinating glimpse into his mind.

He held private meetings in that office with compañeros from all over Latin America to discuss common dreams for the redemption of our continent. Its walls are silent witnesses to many plans reflecting the purest longings of a generation.

As Che's trips became longer, his yearning for home became more acute. During one of his last trips, he made a brief stop in Paris. He sent me a postcard from the Louvre, a portrait of Lucrecia Crivelli painted by Leonardo de Vinci.* On the back he wrote:

---

* This postcard is reproduced in the photo section of this book.

My darling,

I was dreaming of holding your hand in the Louvre, and here you are—a little chubby and serious, with a sad sort of smile (perhaps because no one loves you), waiting for your lover who is far away. (Is it who I'm thinking of, or another?)

I let go of your hand to take a better look at you and to guess what is hidden in the generous breast. A boy? Yes?

Kisses and a huge hug for everyone and a special one for you,

From

Marshal Thu Che

He was in a very creative phase, the product of his years of experience in the revolution and his rigorous personal study program. This is reflected in his speeches and writings from this period, such as his speech in Geneva in March 1964 at the United Nations Conference on Trade and Development and the speech he gave at the UN General Assembly in December of that same year:

> As an underdeveloped Latin American country, [Cuba] will support the main demands of its fraternal countries, and as a country under attack it will denounce from the very outset all the machinations set in train by the coercive apparatus of that imperial power, the United States of America.*

---

* This speech is included in *Che Guevara Reader* (Seven Stories Press, 2022).

At the United Nations, he spoke plainly:

> Cuba comes here to state its position on the most important points of controversy and will do so with the full sense of responsibility that the use of this rostrum implies, while at the same time fulfilling the unavoidable duty of speaking clearly and frankly.
>
> We would like to see this assembly shake itself out of its complacency and move forward. We would like to see the committees begin their work and not stop at the first confrontation. Imperialism wants to turn this meeting into a pointless oratorical tournament, instead of solving the serious problems of the world. We must prevent it from doing so. This session of the assembly should not be remembered in the future solely by the number 19 that identifies it. Our efforts are directed to that end.*

Che was renowned for his strict adherence to revolutionary ethics. In his many trips abroad, his hosts would often give him gifts, sometimes very valuable gifts. He would always give these gifts away to others. This never bothered me, even when the gifts were supposed to be for me as his wife. Instead, he would bring me some exotic piece of fabric or some other object or handicraft from the countries he visited. I still have many of those simple treasures.

Once he gave away a color television that I was sent, at the time when they were almost unattainable. He gave it to a worker within his ministry. At other times, he would share what he received. After a visit to Algeria, for example, he received a barrel of excellent wine. When he got home he told me he was going to distribute it among the soldiers of the garrison next door to

---

* This speech is included in *Che Guevara Reader* (Seven Stories Press, 2022).

our house. I didn't always obey his orders, and I didn't on that occasion. Wine was one of his few pleasures in life, so I put away a few liters of that wine for our household. I don't regret this.

I remember he once sent Fidel some peaches and dates that he had been given because he knew that Fidel had a weakness for them. On the few occasions when he bought me a modest gift, he argued that one should never use the state's money for personal things. But he never failed to send us postcards from the various countries he visited. On one of his last trips, before he left for the Congo in 1965, he wrote to me telling me that, from whatever country he found himself in, he would buy me something, but it wouldn't be the ring with a precious stone he had promised on a previous occasion:

> *My darling,*
>
> *This might be my last letter for some time. I am thinking of you and of the little parts of my flesh I've left behind. This job gives me a lot of time for reflection, in spite of everything.*
>
> *I won't send you the ring because I don't think it's appropriate to spend money on that, especially now that we need the money. But I will send you something from my destination.*
>
> *For the moment, I send you passionate kisses capable of melting your cold heart, and you can divide one kiss into little pieces for the children. Give the in-laws my regards, as well as the rest of the family. To the newlyweds [my niece] I send hugs, and the recommendation that they name the first child Ramón.**

---

* Ramón was Che's *nom de guerre.*

*In the tropical nights I will be returning to my old and
badly executed trade as a poet (not so much in composition
but at least in my mind), and you will be the only
protagonist.*

*Don't give up your studies. Work hard and remember me
now and then.*

A final one, passionate, with no rhetoric, from your

Ramón

When he returned he told me he had thought about buying the
ring, but couldn't bring himself to spend money that was not his
to spend. Instead, when he left for the Congo, he left me his watch,
which had a great sentimental value.

As previously explained, from early on Che resisted all
suggestions (even from Fidel) that I join him on his trips. He
always argued it was a privilege he would not accept. Sometimes
I would have to go to Fidel's office on 11th street to speak to
Che on the phone when he was overseas. He only accepted this
arrangement because it was Fidel's suggestion.

These two men had a truly unique relationship. There were
times when they did not share the same opinion about something.
On those occasions they would argue for hours (or days), finally
coming to some kind of agreement. They were like two parts of a
whole. A boundless trust existed between them, something Che
expressed in his farewell letter to Fidel when he left for the Congo.
He said he had felt proud at being part of the Cuban people and to
be led by a man of Fidel's stature.

I knew Che had big plans, part of a bigger objective, that had
taken root in his mind many years before—from the time when,

as an adolescent, he had set out on a motorbike with his friend Alberto Granado to see and experience the misery and injustice of our continent.* In Cuba, he said, he had found his true vocation. On leaving, he wrote: "I leave here [in Cuba] the purest of my hopes as a builder and the dearest of my loved ones."

Che was aware that Cuba had managed to build an authentic revolution with great effort and much perseverance; moreover, he saw that in Fidel, the Cuban people had a leader who was loved and admired. Che decided to become part of the revolutionary movement that was emerging in the Third World fighting to create a more just and equal world. This decision matured in him as he became more familiar with the liberation movements in different parts of the world. Those movements knew they had Cuba's unconditional support and in Che they found an enthusiastic collaborator.

He saw many valuable leaders being killed in combat, and believed that only with the effective participation of experienced combatants could those liberation movements be victorious. He also believed direct example was crucial and he was prepared to "risk his own skin," as he put it. Those of us who knew him well understood he would not be diverted from this course, although we argued he should wait until conditions were better prepared.

He focused on this broader objective of the liberation of the Third World in his speech in Algeria in February 1965:

> It is not by accident that our [Cuban] delegation is permitted to give its opinion here, in the circle of the peoples of Asia and Africa. A common aspiration unites us in our march toward the future: the defeat of imperialism. A common past of struggle against the same enemy has united us along the road…

---

* Ernesto Che Guevara: *The Motorcycle Diaries: Notes on a Latin American Journey* (Seven Stories Press, 2021).

It is imperative to take political power and to get rid of the oppressor classes. But then the second stage of the struggle, which may be even more difficult than the first, must be faced...

We must fight against imperialism. Each time a country is torn away from the imperialist tree, it is not only a partial battle won against the main enemy but it also contributes to the real weakening of that enemy, and is one more step toward the final victory.*

He decided to go to the Congo, Africa, first.** He had closely followed political developments in Africa, and planned to stay there as long as necessary. He would then return to Latin America to fulfill his long-held dream of achieving the liberation of that continent.

I knew and accepted the enormous risks involved in this, motivated as he was by his sense of duty and also his desire to progress toward his ultimate goal. On a personal level, however, I realized nothing would ever be the same again for us. We spoke about how I could join him when the children would not be so affected by our absence. I held onto the idea that I would follow him as soon as possible. But he argued I had to stay with the children to provide the love, care and guidance that only I could offer them. I had to acknowledge that he was right.

Despite his attempts to calm my fears, I was still shocked when Che told me of his decision to go to the Congo. One Sunday morning, he didn't go to his voluntary work as he usually did.

---

* This speech is included in *Che Guevara Reader* (Seven Stories Press, 2022).

** The Congo won independence from Belgium in 1960, but almost immediately was torn apart by secessionist and imperialist forces. In 1965, Che Guevara left Cuba to lead a group of Cubans assisting the Congolese revolutionary movement.

Instead he stayed at home and we took photographs with the children on the balcony of our house. I didn't think anything of this, because we didn't yet have any photos of our baby son Ernesto, who had been born while Che was in Algeria.

Then he told me he had booked a house at the beach, something he had never done before. But our beach holiday at Bocaciega became a sad memory for me. When the children were in bed and we were alone, he told me he would be leaving soon. I felt as if the world was about to end.

After he left, I'm not entirely sure when, but it might have been the day Fidel publicly announced Che's farewell letter,* Vilma came to the house to give me some letters he had written to the children and to his parents. There was another envelope simply addressed, "Only for you," containing tape recordings of him reading some of the poems we had shared in our intimate moments.

By leaving me those tapes, he wrote, he was leaving the best part of himself, assuring me I was part of his world forever. I just can't describe my feelings when I heard his voice reciting "our poems," poems such as Pablo Neruda's "Adios: Veinte poemas del amor;" "La sangre numerosa," "El abuelo" by Nicolás Guillén; and "La pupila insomne" by Rubén Martínez Villena. I cried uncontrollably, unable to stop. They were tears of joy, but at the same time I was conscious of a gigantic abyss opening inside me.

I have listened to those tapes many times over the years and they always distress me. I always ask myself the same question: Should I have gone with him? As it was, there was nothing I could do but wait, try to maintain my optimism and watch our children grow and thrive. They were truly the fruits of a great love, of our love.

---

* Che's farewell letter was addressed to Fidel, who read it to the first meeting of the newly founded Cuban Communist Party's central committee meeting on October 3, 1965. See *Che Guevara Reader* (Seven Stories Press, 2022).

8

There are times when words are totally inadequate. It is almost impossible for me now to recall what happened, how Che left and my feelings at the time, partly because I always told myself I would never, ever talk about these things.

I do remember feeling that not only would our relationship change but also that I would never be the same again. When we parted, we assumed that communication would be slow and irregular, but thankfully this was not the case. In the first few months Che was in the Congo, we wrote to each other regularly, and that helped dissipate the uncertainty I felt. There were many compañeros who acted as emissaries, taking and delivering our letters. Osmany Cienfuegos, José Ramón Machado Ventura, Ulíses Estrada, Fernández Mell and Emilio Aragonés were some of those who traveled back and forth from Cuba to the Congo, or who were part of Che's unit.

These letters remain among my most precious possessions, and reading them shows I wasn't the only one being tested by our separation. Che, too, experienced great pain. I, at least, had the company of our children, and gained some consolation from them as the testimony of our love.

When I reread these letters now, so many years after they arrived from that distant land of the Congo, I can see the enormous sacrifice it was for Che to leave us behind.

His first letter sent from the Congo began:

> *To my only one in the world,*
>
> *(I've borrowed this phrase from old Hickmet)**
>
> *What miracles you have performed with my poor old shell. I no longer want a real hug and I dream of the concave space in which you comfort me, your smell and your rough rural caresses.*
>
> *This is another Sierra Maestra, but without the same sense of constructing something or the satisfaction of making it my own. Everything happens very slowly here, as if war was something to be done the day after next. For now, your fear of me being killed is as unfounded as your feelings of jealousy.*
>
> *My work involves teaching several classes of French every day, learning Swahili and providing medical care. Within a few days I will begin the serious work of training. A sort of Minas del Frio from the war, not the one we visited together.*
>
> *Give a tender kiss to each child (including Hildita).*
>
> *Take a photo with all of them and send it to me. Not too big and another little one. Study French in preference to nursing and love me.*
>
> *A long kiss, like our kiss when we are reunited.*
>
> *I love you,*
>
> *Tatu*

---

* The Turkish poet Nazim Hickmet was one of Che's favorite poets.

He used the pseudonym *Tatu*, meaning "three" in Swahili, during his time in Africa. While I waited for him, I focused on the children, who were all very little, as well as my work in the FMC. I resisted taking any long-term responsibility in the FMC in order to be free to join Che when circumstances permitted.

He constantly expressed his pain at our separation, but asked me not to despair. He urged me to study French so that I could function more effectively if I went to the Congo. Although I tried to fill the void as best I could, I never really came to terms with life without Che.

While he was in the Congo, Che learned of the death of his mother, which affected him deeply, as they had been very close. In a sorrowful letter, he expressed the hope "she had not suffered physically and hopefully she hadn't had time to think about me."

He wrote one his most moving stories ("The Stone") in memory of his mother. In it, he poured out his sense of loss, feeling "a physical need for my mother to be here so that I can rest my head in her bony lap. I need to hear her call me her 'dear old fella' with such tenderness, to feel her clumsy hand in my hair, caressing me in strokes, like a rag doll, the tenderness streaming from her eyes and voice, the broken channels no longer bearing it to the extremities. Her hands tremble and touch rather than caress, but the tenderness still flows from them. I feel so good, so small, so strong. There is no need to ask her for forgiveness. She understands everything. This is evident in her words 'my dear old fella'..."*

This was the man whom some people thought severe. I knew him more intimately. Sometimes he had to show he was firm, although at the same time he could be tender and affectionate. When I pleaded with him to let me come and join him, he replied:

---

* Che's short story, "The Stone," is included as an appendix to this book.

Don't try to blackmail me. You can't come now or in three months' time. Maybe in a year it will be different and then we'll see. This has to be properly analyzed. The most important thing is that when you come you aren't "the little wife" but rather a combatant. You must be prepared for that, at least in French...

A good part of my life has been like that: having to hold back the love I feel for other considerations. That's why I might be regarded as a mechanical monster. Help me now Aleida, be strong, and don't create problems that can't be resolved. When we married, you knew who I was. You must do your part so that the road is easier; there is still a long road ahead.

Love me passionately, but with understanding; my path is laid out and nothing but death will stop me. Don't feel sad for me; grab hold of life and make the best of it. Some journeys we will be able to take together. What drives me has nothing to do with a casual thirst for adventure and what that entails. I know that, and so should you. [...]

Educate the children. Don't spoil them or pamper them too much, especially Camilo. Don't think of abandoning them because it isn't fair. They are part of us.

I give you a long and sweet embrace,

Your Tatu

Was I as strong as Che wanted me to be? I didn't know for sure. Sometimes I felt like Dulcinea and at other times like Sancho Panza in my desire to follow the Quixote of modern times, with whom I had chosen to share my life. Like the fictional Quixote,

Che was full of tenderness but he never hesitated in challenging new windmills.

I resigned myself to the wait. Events in the Congo, however, took an unexpected turn.* Despite this, Che tried his best to keep the revolutionary forces intact. He maintained his personal discipline in his application to his intensive study program. He increased the number of books he requested, broadening his reading list. It is extraordinary how, in the midst of all the problems and hardships he experienced in the Congo, and the growing sense of disaster, he continued to study philosophy and other subjects he thought would help him understand better how the Third World could achieve socialism. He constantly asked me for more books; the list speaks for itself. Along with the titles that he requested, he often added comments in brackets:

Hymns Triumphant by Pindar

Tragedies by Aeschylus

Dramas and Tragedies by Sophocles

Dramas and Tragedies by Euripides

Complete Comedies by Aristophanes

The Histories by Herodotus

Greek History by Xenophon

Political Speeches by Demosthenes

Dialogues by Plato

The Republic by Plato

Politics by Aristotle (especially this one)

Parallel Lives by Plutarch

---

* See Ernesto Che Guevara: *Congo Diary: Episodes of the Revolutionary War in the Congo* (Seven Stories Press, 2021).

Don Quixote of La Mancha

Complete Works by Racine

The Divine Comedy by Dante

Orlando Furious by Ariosto

Faust by Goethe

Complete Works by Shakespeare

Exercises in Analytical Geometry (from my sanctuary)

Despite his best efforts, the struggle in the Congo came to an unsuccessful conclusion. I received a letter from Che written in Tanzania on November 28, 1965, in which he explained what had happened, how he felt about it and his future plans. He tried to make me see a reunion would be very difficult at that time:

My darling,

Your last letter arrived. Everything turned out differently from what we had expected. Osmany can tell you about the sequence of events. I can only say that my troop made me proud; almost immediately, it became diluted, or rather, melted like lard in a fry pan, escaping from my grasp. I am returning, along the road of defeat, with an army of shadows. Now everything is over and the time has come for the last stage of my journey—the definitive one. Only a handful of select men will come with me—those with stars on their foreheads (the stars of Martí, not military ones).

Our separation was always going to be a long one. I had hoped to be able to see you during what I thought would be a long war, but it wasn't possible. Now there will be a lot of hostile territory between us, and communication will be less frequent. I can't see you before I leave because I must avoid all possibility of being detected. In the mountains I felt secure, with my weapon in my hand, but I don't feel in my element in clandestinity. I have to be extra cautious.

Now comes the truly difficult time for everyone, and we must be prepared to bear it. I hope you know how. You must bear your cross with revolutionary fervor. If I reach my destination, and when they realize it, they will do everything to destroy us. Our security measures will then need to be even more rigid, and we will have to accept a greater isolation. I will always find ways to get a few lines to you; but if I can't, please don't imagine the worst. I will regain my spirits once I reach my destination, even though there will be problems at first.

It is hard for me to write this. The technical details are of no interest and memories of a past life will take time to recover. You know I'm a combination of adventurer and bourgeois, with a terrible yearning to come home, while at the same time, anxious to realize my dreams. When I was in my bureaucratic cave, I dreamed of doing what I have begun to do. Now, and for the rest of my journey, I will dream of you, while the children inevitably grow up. They must have such a strange vision of me. How difficult it will be for them one day to love me like a father and not regard me as some distant monster they are obliged to love.

When I leave, I will leave you some books and notes, please keep them. I have become so accustomed to reading and studying, it is now second nature to me—a great contrast to my adventurous spirit. As always, I wrote you a little

*verse and, as always, I tore it up. I am a better critic and
I don't want accidents like the last time. Now that I am a
prisoner, with no enemies nearby, or injustices in my sights,
my need for you is virulent and physiological, and cannot
always be calmed by Karl Marx or Vladimir Ilyich.*

*Give the birthday girl a special kiss. I haven't sent her
anything because it is better for me to disappear altogether.
I saw you standing on a platform; you looked really great,
almost like in the good old days of Santa Clara. I, too, was
almost restored to my former self, but now I am once again
the insignificant Bald Samson.*

*Educate the children. I always worry about the boys, in
particular. Tell the old man to visit them. Give a big hug to
the good old folks you have there and receive an embrace
yourself—not the last one, but with all my love and the
desperation as if it was our last embrace.*

A kiss,

Ramón

At this time, Fidel, who was always checking on our family,
invited me to participate at the first graduation ceremony of
doctors after the revolution. This was held at Turquino, the
highest mountain in Cuba, situated in the Sierra Maestra.

The symbolism of the place was very strong, and many
important events were held there. On arrival, we saw Sergio del
Valle, an aide-de-camp and doctor in Camilo Cienfuegos's Second
Column, who was then chief of staff of the armed forces. He
had come to tell Fidel about the withdrawal of Che's troop from
the Congo, which Che explained in greater detail in his letter to

Fidel. Che wrote a comprehensive analysis of the experience in the Congo while he was in Tanzania, based on the diary he had kept. This has now been published as *Congo Diary: Episodes of the Revolutionary War in the Congo*. As soon as we knew the Cubans had withdrawn from the Congo, Fidel gave me permission to go and see Che. He acted as mediator between us as he had done in the past. I fervently hoped Che wouldn't resist, and to my delight, this time he didn't. My trip to Tanzania was confirmed in December 1965, making me extraordinarily happy. As I prepared for my departure, I decided this was the most eagerly awaited New Year celebration of my life.

Sometime around January 15, 1966, I landed in Prague. I stayed in an apartment that would later be used by Che and other compañeros while they prepared for their Latin America mission. I had traveled with Juan Carretero (*Ariel*), a compañero from the department of the Cuban Communist Party, headed by the legendary "Red Beard" (Manual Piñeiro), one of the key coordinators of Cuba's links with the revolutionary movements in Latin America. From Prague, we traveled to Cairo and then on to Tanzania.

Che was waiting for me there, transformed into another character I almost didn't recognize. He was clean shaven, not wearing the olive green uniform he always wore in Cuba. I, too, was incognito, extremely nervous, full of doubts. But all that vanished as soon as I recognized him and we were together again.

In order to travel, I had disguised myself with a black wig and glasses that made me look much older than I was. So two apparent strangers met in Tanzania, but our feelings for each other could not be disguised.

For a short time, we were able to be completely alone. Our solitary confinement was necessary for security reasons, but we couldn't have been happier. I had a chance to look around the city briefly when I arrived and again when I left. Our accommodation was not particularly comfortable, but that hardly mattered. We had a single room in which we slept, ate and studied, and a bathroom, where Che developed some of the photographs he had taken with his professional quality camera. We also returned to our regular routine. After breakfast, I would read, always with Che's guidance, and he would read or write. He also gave me French lessons, and I made some progress.

During this time in Tanzania he recorded himself reading stories for the children. These recordings became some of their most valued possessions. He also wrote Fidel a letter, asking me to deliver it. This was an analysis of the liberation movement in Guatemala.

We discussed many things. I remember his comments about his farewell letter to Fidel, and how important it was to him. He was clear, wherever he went to fight after the Congo, that he would always regard himself as representing the Cuban revolution, symbolized in the battle-cry: *"Hasta la victoria siempre! Patria o muerte!"* [Until victory, always! Homeland or death!]

Not everything was serious, of course. We reminisced about happy times and things we had experienced in our lives together. We also cleared up a few past misunderstandings, including the incident in the INRA office with the disappearing secretary. He said he had always thought I had asked her to leave because her role was superfluous, as I took care of all his personal affairs. Every time we had discussed this before, I denied my role. But now, after six years, I finally confessed. I explained it was not because I was jealous, or that I had a bad opinion of the young woman, but because, from a political point of view, I didn't believe she was up to the task of being Che's secretary. Che was satisfied with this explanation.

We discussed our friends, for example what had happened to my friend Lolita Rosell, to whom I had been close during our time in the underground struggle. After the revolution, Lolita became president of the FMC in Las Villas. She had some difficulties in her province with the sectarian faction in the party, led by Aníbal Escalante. She requested a meeting with Che to discuss this. He agreed on the condition that a number of others also attend the meeting. These were: Emilio Aragones, a member of the PURS* and the head of the army in Las Villas; William Gálvez and a leader of the former PSP, compañero Luzardo, who was then Minister of Interior Commerce. I never heard about what had happened at that meeting, but Lolita told me she was happy with the outcome. In Tanzania, Che told me how Lolita had shown great integrity and courage. After that meeting, Che asked her to come to Havana to work in the newly created Ministry of the Sugar Industry.

Che's next plans were becoming urgent. In spite of what had happened in the Congo, he still intended to proceed with his plan to extend the struggle for the liberation of Latin America, following in the footsteps of Simón Bolívar and José Martí.

I don't quite remember when he left for Prague—maybe my mind refused to register it—but I think it was in the first few weeks of March. I found myself alone in the little room that had been our refuge. I was devastated, and not even reading distracted me. I hardly understood what I was reading.

Maybe I should have written down my thoughts but I couldn't. I feared I would never see Che again, or maybe not for many years. I knew that I had to get used to the idea and live with the feeling that it might have been our last time together. We had several separations like this, and each time felt like it was final.

---

* The United Party of Socialist Revolution (PURS) developed out of the Integrated Revolutionary Organizations (ORI). It was the forerunner of the Cuban Communist Party that was formed in 1965.

I always expected my life to be full of anxiety and uncertainty. This time, after experiencing such peace and pleasure at being reunited, I dreaded to think I might never hear from Che again. While he had been in the Congo we were able to communicate once a month. But now?

I returned to Cuba having been away for a month and half. I traveled from Cairo to Moscow with Oscar Fernández Padilla. My despairing mood was somewhat brightened when I was reunited with my children and able to give them the special gift of the tape-recorded stories read by their father.

A few days later Fidel's office called, asking me to pick up a small notebook Che had sent me along with some personal notes. One of the pieces in the notebook was titled "Delivery," reflecting the sadness and certainty he felt at the prospect we would not see each other for a long time:

My love,

The moment has come to send you a farewell tasting of earth (dry leaves, something far away and disused). I wanted to do this with lines that don't reach the margins— often called poems—but I have failed.

There are so many intimate things for your ears only that words cannot express, only the shy algorithms that amuse my breaking wave. The noble trade of poet is not for me. It isn't that I don't have sweet things to say. If you only knew what is contained there in a whirl inside me. But the shell that contains them is too long, convoluted and narrow. They emerge, exhausted from the journey, and in a bad mood, elusive; the sweetest ones are the most fragile and are left behind, shattered, disparate vibrations...

I'm a useless medium. I would disintegrate trying to convey everything at once. Let's use everyday words to capture the moment.

[...] That is how I love you, remembering the bitter coffee every morning, the taste of the dimple in your knee, the ash of a cigar delicately balanced, the incoherent grumbling with which you defend your impregnable pillow.[...]

That is how I love you, watching the children grow, like a staircase with no history (and I suffer because I can't witness those steps). Every day, it's like a stabbing in my side, upbraiding the idler from its shell.

This will be a real farewell. Five years in the mire have aged me. Now there remains only one last step—the definitive one.

The siren songs have ended, and so has my inner conflict. Now the flag is raised for my last race. The speed will be such that screams will accompany me. The past has come to an end; I am the future in progress.

Don't call me, because I won't be able to hear you. But I will sense you on sunny days, under the renewed caress of bullets. [...]

I will keep a look out for you, in the way a dog remains alert while it's resting, and I will imagine every part of you, piece by piece, and altogether.

If one day you feel the force of an overbearing presence, don't turn around, don't break the spell, just keep on preparing my coffee, and let me experience you in that instant, for always.

It so happened that fortune smiled on us again. After my constant complaints and Che's continued resistance, in April 1966 we were reunited in Prague. In this undated letter, he wrote:

> *Two letters. It isn't true that I don't want to see you and I have not run away [...].*
>
> *I came here to get things going and that is what has happened to some extent. I didn't think it was appropriate for you to come. You might have been detected (by the Czechs or our enemies). Your absence from Cuba would be noticed immediately. Moreover, travel is expensive and this upsets me. If Fidel wants you to come, then that's up to him (he can weigh up the factors) and he can decide [...].*

Prague was an enchanting city; but the fact that we didn't have much of an opportunity to enjoy it fully didn't matter to us. We had to maintain strict discipline, functioning in absolute secrecy. It was enough for us to simply be together again.

We stayed in two places in that beautiful city: one was the apartment I had stayed in on my way to Tanzania. It was quite small, with only one room with a bed, and a bathroom that was also used as a kitchen and laundry. We stayed there for a week.

Then we moved to a large, comfortable country house. The owner lived there with her daughter, who had an intellectual disability. They cooked for us and we were there with other compañeros who were preparing to go to Bolivia with Che. These were Alberto Fernández Montes de Oca (*Pacho*), Harry Villegas (*Pombo*) and Carlos Coello (*Tuma*) and others, who visited for work reasons.

At night we played canasta to entertain ourselves. I didn't

particularly enjoy those card games because I always lost. Che would try to help me—whenever I was in a tight spot he came to my rescue. He was the same when we had target practice. He would stand behind me to correct my stance, never allowing me to look bad in any situation where I was being tested. This was his way of showing me his affection and support.

I could only ever manage to beat Coello in target practice. He was less dexterous than I was and a terrible shot. We enjoyed his jokes and his cheerful personality. We were all very fond of him. I would joke with him, saying I would take his place in the next struggle, repeating this often to see if anyone was paying attention.

If the day was fine, we would go on walks through a nearby pine forest; at weekends, we would return to the city at night with José Luis Ojalvo, the compañero who looked after us in Prague.

On odd occasions, we would break the rules and escape. Once we went to eat at a restaurant close to the apartment, and an amusing incident occurred. We generally ordered beef steak, and Che would put on his best Czech accent. But on that occasion, we wanted to try something different. Confident of his ability in French, Che ordered for us. We were very surprised when the waiter brought us "bistec anglisqui"—what we always ordered. We laughed so much at the waiter's perfect French. We were happy, enjoying our time alone together and our adventures with the others. Once we went to a stadium to watch a game of soccer.

I especially remember a day trip we made to a rural area. On our return we stayed in a small, very friendly motel. There, we let ourselves dream a bit, making plans to return some day. But this was never possible. Yet again we had to forego our small pleasures. Similarly, we never got to see Karlovy Vary, a beautiful spa town Che very much wanted us to visit together.

At the end of May we learned of a possible attack on Cuba by the United States, following the assassination of one of our soldiers guarding the Guantánamo Naval Base, territory usurped by the United States from the time of Cuba's so-called independence in 1902.

Due to the seriousness of the situation, Che brought forward the date of my departure, originally scheduled for June 2, the date of our wedding anniversary. I would be lying if I said I was happy to return. But of course I wanted to be with my children and had little choice in the matter. Che decided, in the case of a US attack against Cuba, he would return to Cuba to fight alongside his people.

The day before I left, I went to a store and bought him some cuff links to surprise him. They were quite small, and I knew he would always be able to carry them with him; and I believe he did, because no one has ever returned them to me. (It's possible someone has held onto them as a war trophy.) He never knew the cuff links were a gift from me until he returned to Cuba in July 1966 to train the group that would go to Bolivia. He was then overjoyed.

Che had not considered returning to Cuba after the Congo mission. Again, he was convinced by Fidel's great power of persuasion. Fidel wrote to Che in Prague, arguing that Cuba was the best place to complete the final phase of the training for Bolivia, assuring him of his total discretion:

Dear Ramón:

Events have overtaken my plans for a letter [...]

It seems to me, given the delicate and worrying situation in which you find yourself there, that you should consider the usefulness of jumping back here.

I am well aware that you are especially reluctant to consider any option that involves a return to Cuba for the moment, unless it is in the quite exceptional circumstances mentioned above.

But analyzed in a sober and objective way, this actually hinders your objectives; worse, it puts them at risk. I find it very hard to accept the idea that this is right, or even that it can be justified from a revolutionary point of view. Your time at the so-called halfway point increases the risks; it makes extraordinarily more difficult the practical tasks that need to be carried out; and far from accelerating the plans, it delays their fulfillment; moreover, it subjects you to a period of unnecessarily anxious, uncertain and impatient waiting.

What can be the point of that? There is no question of principle, honor or revolutionary morality involved here that would prevent you from making effective and thorough use of facilities that you can certainly depend on to achieve your goal. No fraud, no deception, no tricking of the people of Cuba or the world is involved in making use of the objective advantages of being able to enter and leave here, to plan and coordinate, to select and train cadres, and to do everything from here that you can achieve only with great difficulty from where you are or somewhere similar. Neither today nor tomorrow, nor at any time in the future, could anyone consider it wrong—nor should you in all conscience. What would really be a grave, unforgivable error is to do things badly when they could be done well; to have a failure when all the possibilities are there for success.

*I am not insinuating, not in the least, that you abandon
or postpone your plans, nor am I letting myself be carried
away by pessimistic considerations due to the difficulties
that have arisen. On the contrary, the difficulties can be
overcome, and more than ever we can count on having the
experience, the conviction and the means to carry out those
plans successfully. That is why I think we should make the
best and most rational use of the knowledge, the resources
and the facilities that we have at our disposal. Since first
hatching your now old idea of further action in another
setting, have you ever really had enough time to devote
yourself entirely to this matter, to conceiving, organizing
and executing your plans to the greatest possible extent?
[...]*

*It is a huge advantage for you to be able to use what
we have here, to have access to houses, isolated farms,
mountains, cays and everything essential to organize and
personally lead the project, devoting 100 percent of your
time to this and drawing on the help of as many others
as necessary, with only a very small number of people
knowing your whereabouts. You know perfectly well that
you can count on these facilities, that there is not the
slightest possibility that you will encounter problems
or interference for reasons of state or politics. The most
difficult thing of all—the official disassociation—has
already been done, not without paying a price in the form of
slander, intrigues, etc. Is it right that we should not extract
the maximum benefit from it? Has any revolutionary ever
had such ideal conditions to fulfill their mission, and at*

a time when that mission acquires great importance for humanity, when the most crucial and decisive struggle for the victory of the peoples is breaking out? [...]

Why not do things well if we have every chance to do so? Why don't we take the minimum time necessary, even while working at the greatest speed? [...]

I hope these lines won't annoy or upset you. I know that if you analyze what I say seriously, your characteristic honesty will lead you to accept that I am right. But even if you come to a completely different decision, I won't feel disappointed. I write to you with deep affection and the greatest and most sincere admiration for your brilliant and noble intelligence, your irreproachable conduct and your unyielding character of a whole-hearted revolutionary. The fact that you might see things differently won't change these feelings one iota nor affect our collaboration in any way.*

I have always regarded this letter as testimony to the incredible bond of loyalty and respect that existed between these two men, two intransigent guerrilla fighters — an eloquent answer to the many lies and slanders spread about them.

I received a brief note from Che addressed to my *nom de guerre*. He reproached me for tearing out the page of his copy of *El Ciervo* on which the author, the Spanish poet León Felipe, had written a dedication to him:

Josephine, my love,

---

* For the full text of this letter, see Ernesto Che Guevara: *Congo Diary: Episodes of the Revolutionary War in the Congo* (Seven Stories Press, 2021).

I will soon experience another warm and salty shower,
related to my clandestine status.**

You have mutilated my copy of El Ciervo *and I cannot*
forgive you. If I get the chance, I'll take my revenge.

A warm kiss, because it is very new and full of hope.
Another big one for the children.

Your Ramón

Che returned to Cuba around the time of the July 26 celebrations when many visitors were arriving at the airport, making it less likely he would be identified by journalists. But as always there was a slight hitch. When he arrived, Santiago Alvarez had a crew filming the arrival of various celebrities. Two compañeros from Piñeiro's office, Juan Carretero and Armando Campos, had to intervene and go to ICAIC to ensure that the film was destroyed.

Many years later, Santiago, a well-known documentary film maker, enjoyed narrating the story of how the two men had come to his studio and asked to see the film shot at the airport. With so many reels of film to watch, the search took a very long time. Moreover, poor Santiago didn't know what they were looking for. Eventually, they found the images of Che in disguise, and those sections were cut from the reel. This remained a secret for decades.

In my view, this was probably unnecessary, because Che was totally unrecognizable. Before leaving Prague, he put on thick glasses and padding around his body, which made him look corpulent and slightly hunched over; he generally appeared much older than he was.

I can't remember if it was that same day that Celia Sánchez

---

* A reference to the fact that Che was expecting to return to Cuba.

called to tell me she would pick me up in a few minutes. If I wanted to, she said, I could bring Ernesto with me, our youngest child, whom Che had hardly had a chance to get to know. He was only one month old when Che left for the Congo. I didn't need to be told where I was going.

I collected a few essential items while I waited for Celia to pick me up in her car. This was my first visit to San Andrés de Caiguanabo in Pinar del Río, an extraordinarily beautiful place Fidel had selected for the training of the small group of combatants that would accompany Che to Bolivia.

I had to return home the next day, because my prolonged absence would provoke rumors or questions. I was told I could return whenever circumstances allowed. At this point, it was critical that nothing should get in the way of the plans.

None of that worried me, of course, and I enjoyed our clandestine encounters. The most important thing for me was to have him nearby, away from danger and among compañeros and friends, beyond the reach of an enemy bullet or a breach of security that would undermine his project.

I traveled to see him whenever I could. Sometimes I stayed a bit longer, and Che allowed me to take part in the training exercises with the other compañeros. We went for long hikes in the strong sun; the men would be encumbered with their backpacks and weapons, and I would be as free as the wind, following Che as in the old days.

Sometimes we would compete with the rest of the group to see who arrived back first at the starting point. Che usually walked slowly, but without stopping to rest, and if we did stop, we did not sit down. In that way, we left many compañeros behind.

In August, I took little Celia with me. She was only three years old and was sick with a sore throat. Che was delighted to see her

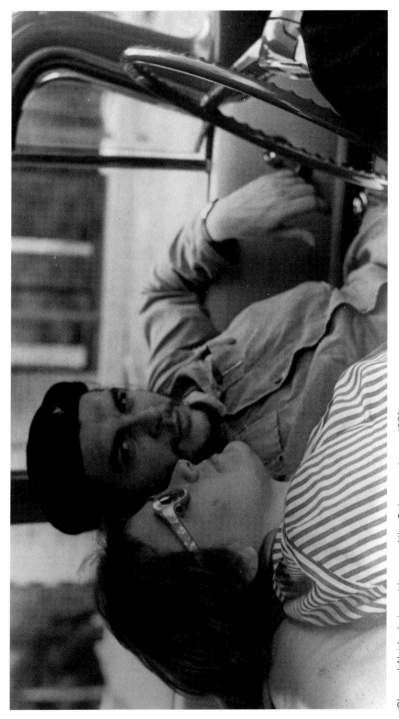

Che and Aleida during a trip around the Cuban provinces, 1959.

Aleida and Che organizing their office in their Nuevo Vedado home, 1963.

With Camilo, Che and Aleida's first-born son.

At the wedding of Aleida's niece Miriam Moya March, 1965.

With Ernestico (Ernesto) their second son, in 1965.

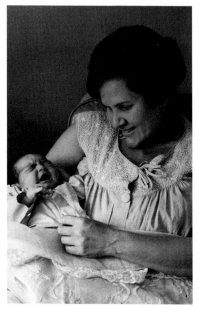

With Celia, their third child, in 1964.

February 1965, with the newborn Ernesto.

With Fidel at a 1965 ceremony in Revolution Plaza.

Almendares Park, December 1964. Left to right: Camilo, Celia, Aleida and Aleidita.

March 1965, in front of their house in Nuevo Vedado, Havana, before Che left for the Congo. Children (from left): Ernesto, Camilo, Aleidita and Celia.

July 1965. From left: Aleida and Ernesto, Camilo, Hildita (Che's daughter with Hilda Gadea) and Aleidita.

Musée du Louvre (École Florentine).

A postcard with a portrait of Lucrecia Crivelli, Che sent to Aleida from the Louvre Museum, Paris. in 1965.

This 1965 family photo was sent to Che in the Congo.

Aleida with Fidel and Rosa E. Navarro at the end of 1965 at Turquino Peak, in the Sierra Maestra mountains.

Lunch at the home of Cuban Foreign Minister Raúl Roa (left).

January 1966: Aleida and Che disguised as Josefina and Ramón, during their meeting in Tanzania after Che had been in the Congo, Africa. (Photos taken by Che.)

Aleida with Che in Tanzania. (Photo taken by Che.)

Tanzania. (Photo taken by Che.)

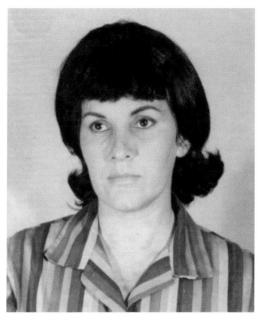

Aleida's passport photo as Josefina González, January 1966.

The children with Che disguised as "old uncle Ramón" in Havana, October 1966, before he left for Bolivia.

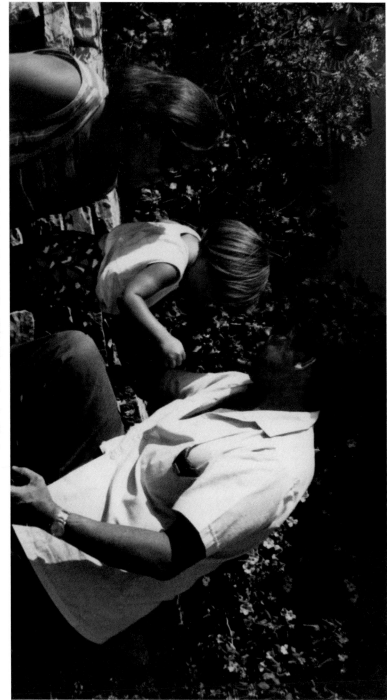

Che, Aleida and their daughter Celia in San Andrés, Pinar del Río, 1966. (Photo taken by Che.)

Aleida with Celia, 1966. (Photo taken by Che.)

Che with Celia in San Andrés, Pinar del Río, 1966.

A rest break during training for Bolivia in San Andrés, Pinar del Río, 1966. (Photo taken by Che.)

With Che disguised as "old uncle Ramón" a few days before he left for Bolivia in 1966.

Family photo taken by Korda in May 1965. Children (from left to right): Hildita (Che's daughter with Hilda Gadea), Aleidita, Camilo, baby Ernesto and Celia.

Aleida with the children, 1966.

The children with their grandparents Juan and Eudoxia on Ernesto's birthday, February 1968.

Aleida as a Cuban representative of the Inter-Parliamentary Group.

The children with their grandmother Eudoxia (Aleida's mother).

Aleida with Fidel at Aleidita's wedding.

Aleida with her friend Ernestina Mazón, her daughter Aleidita and some of her grandchildren.

Daughter Celia's wedding.

Che and Aleida in Santiago de las Vegas, Cuba, 1959.

and enjoyed playing with her, even though she was unaware she was with her father. We took some beautiful photographs that day. In the last letter he wrote to the children, sent for Aliucha's birthday, he wrote, "Celita, help your grandmother around the house and stay as lovely as you were when we said good-bye, do you remember? I bet you do."

On one of our hikes in the mountains of Pinar del Río, as we descended a cliff, the rock I was holding onto came away and I fell backwards, landing about half a meter from the edge. Che quickly came to my rescue. Luckily, I only sustained a few scratches and we continued on our way, arriving back before the rest of the group. When they passed the spot where the accident had occurred and saw blood stains on the rocks, the compañeros became concerned. But they started joking around when they found us sitting waiting for them.

On another occasion, we went out at sunset on horseback with some compañeros. My horse suddenly slipped and I found myself hanging from a small tree, very close to a precipice. Somehow, the horse fell into the ravine. When he saw what had happened, Che had to rescue me again. He checked that I wasn't injured, except for some scratches and torn pants, and went off to rescue the horse. I returned to the house on his horse.

To test the effectiveness of his transformation into "Ramón,"* Che went to visit a group of his former soldiers. I wasn't allowed to go with him, because they might then guess the identity of the stranger. So I stayed hidden behind a window in order to watch their reactions. Che was introduced as a Spanish instructor, a friend of Cuba. No one recognized him, even though he told some jokes, until one of them, Jesús Suárez Gayol, realized it was indeed Che.

---

* Che disguised himself as an older man and used a passport in the name of Ramón Benítez for his clandestine trip to Bolivia to initiate the guerrilla struggle in Latin America.

Their faces reflected the euphoria they experienced, knowing that the troop would be led by their leader. It was a small, select group, many of whom had faithfully collaborated with Che, not only in war but also in the greater struggle, which was the construction of a new society. Some, like Octavio de la Concepción de la Pedraja (*Moro*) and Israel Zayas (*Braulio*) had been with Che in the Congo. Others, including José M. Martínez Tamayo (*Papi*), Harry Villegas (*Pombo*) and Carlos Coello (*Tuma*), were already in La Paz, preparing conditions for the arrival of the rest of group, those "with stars on their foreheads," as Che described these most dedicated and courageous men.*

While the training proceeded in San Andrés, I sometimes cooked for the entire group and this brought everyone together as a happy family. A bit of affection and unity are always important in such moments. I particularly recall *Moro*. He was a little overweight and trying to diet; sometimes he would only get popcorn to eat. But when he saw the others feasting on what I had prepared, he abandoned his diet and ignored the many jokes made at his expense.

On some nights, when we weren't too tired, we watched movies — usually westerns, because that's what everyone liked. Those gatherings were often marred by the presence of hundreds of little frogs. I have always had an irrational fear of frogs. One time, one of them landed on my leg and Vilo Acuna (*Joaquín*) heroically came to my aid. It is strange how in extreme circumstances, we can overcome our fears. During my time as a guerrilla in the Escambray Mountains and in the actual training sessions at Pinar del Río, I was never bothered by those little animals.

---

* Of all the Cubans who joined Che in Bolivia, only Harry Villegas and two others survived.

A select group of compañeros came to visit at the farm. I remember Armando Hart sitting at the dinner table with Che for hours, discussing philosophy or arguing about Sigmund Freud's theories. These discussions were prompted by Che's letter to Armando (Minister for Education) in December 1965, in which he outlined a study guide on Marxism:

> *My dear secretary,*
>
> *My congratulations for the opportunity they have given you to be God: you have six days.** *
>
> *Before you finish and sit down to rest (unless you choose the wise road of the God before you, who rested earlier), I want to propose a few small ideas about developing the culture of our vanguard and our people in general.*
>
> *In this long vacation period I have had my nose buried in philosophy, something I have wanted to do for some time. I came across the first problem: nothing is published in Cuba, if we exclude the hefty Soviet manuals, which have the drawback of not allowing you to think for yourself, because the party has already done it for you, and you just have to digest it. In terms of methodology, it is as anti-Marxist as can be and, moreover, the books tend to be very bad.*
>
> *Second, and no less important, was my ignorance of philosophical language (I fought hard with Master Hegel, and in the first round bit the dust twice). So I made a study plan for myself, which I think could be looked at and improved a lot, but it might constitute the basis for a real*

---

* Armando Hart had just been appointed organization secretary of the newly formed Cuban Communist Party.

school of thought. We have achieved a lot, but someday we will have to think for ourselves. My idea is a reading plan, naturally, but it could be expanded to bringing our serious works into the party publishing house.

[...]

This is a gigantic job, but Cuba deserves it, and I think it can be attempted. I won't bother you any further with this chatter. I've written to you because I don't know much about the people who are presently responsible for ideological work and it may not be prudent to write to them, for other reasons (not just ideological parrotry, which also counts).

Okay, illustrious colleague (in the philosophical sense), I wish you success. I hope we can meet on the seventh day. A hug to the huggables, including one from me to your dear and feisty better half.*

R.**

03

The days of preparing for Bolivia were coming to an end, and this time I resisted Che's departure less, perhaps because I had participated in some of the activities and also because I imagined a reunion would not be too far off. I expected a long struggle,

---

* Haydee Santamaría was Armando Hart's wife.

** The full text of this letter is included in *Ernesto Che Guevara: Self-Portrait* (Ocean Press, 2004).

and I thought we might face five years of separation, but I firmly believed we would be reunited again. That is how I thought when Che left for Bolivia in October 1966.

Over the years, I have always dreaded the advent of the month of October because for Cubans, and for me in particular, this month does not bring good memories, and to describe my feelings is almost impossible.

When everything was ready for Bolivia, I asked, as I had done when he left for the Congo, if he should not stay for another year to complete some tasks that he had previously been assigned. But nothing would detain him. He was convinced that the pillars of the Cuban revolution were strong and he didn't believe his presence in Cuba was essential. In Latin America, however, he saw there was much to be done, and he was eager to contribute to eliminating the evils that had prevailed there for centuries.

A few days before Che's departure, with him now transformed into the old man "Ramón," we went to a safe house in Havana, where he asked to see the children. It had to be that way because he feared that our older children might tell someone if they recognized him, and this could be a serious problem.

When the children arrived, I introduced them to a man I said was a Uruguayan friend of their father and who wanted to meet them. They could never have imagined that this man, who looked as though he was in his 60s, was their father. It was a difficult moment for us both, especially painful for Che because he loved his children but could not say much or treat them in the way he wanted to. This was one of the hardest tests he ever had to undergo.

For the children, it was a most enjoyable day. They played and did their best to amuse their father's friend. They wanted to show him all the clever things they could do, even playing the piano for him, although it sounded more like banging to me. While she was running about, Aleidita, the eldest, hit her head, and Che went over to tend to her. He treated her so tenderly that, a little while later, she came up to me to tell me a secret: "Mommy, that man is in love with me!" Che heard her whisper to me. Neither of us could speak; we just became pale, overwhelmed by emotion.

He left for the airport from that house. He traveled first to Europe and then proceeded to his final destination, La Paz, Bolivia. Before he left, he wrote me a poem that I was told he wanted to write on a white handkerchief, but he couldn't find one. The important thing is this time he did not tear up his poem, and he finally finished what he had long promised me. I hardly need to say I treasure this poem as one of the most cherished mementos Che left me. The final stanza reads:

> *Farewell, my only one,*
> *do not tremble before the hungry wolves*
> *nor in the cold steppes of absence;*
> *I take you with me in my heart*
> *and we will continue together until the road vanishes…*

I wondered if we would experience yet another cycle of separation and reunion. I cried so much on the way home. I remember that I looked over some articles of clothing of Eliseo Reyes (*Rolando*) with the aim of removing any tags that could identify him as Cuban in preparing for his departure for Bolivia. I was searching for anything to do to ease my anguish. I had to get on and face life until I heard any news.

Once again there was uncertainty. News from Bolivia always came through a third person. The only letter I received was via the Peruvian Juan Pablo Chang (*Chino*), after his visit to the Ñancahuasú camp on December 2, 1966, and before he joined the guerrilla unit:

To my only one,

*I take advantage of a friend's trip to send you these words.
They could be posted, but it is more intimate to use the
"unofficial" route. I could say that I miss you to the point
where I can no longer sleep, but I know you wouldn't believe
me, so I won't tell you that. There are days when I feel so
homesick, it takes a complete hold over me. Especially at
Christmas and New Year, you can't imagine how much I
miss your ritual tears, under a star-filled sky that reminds
me how little I have taken from life in a personal sense [...].*

*I can say nothing interesting about my life here. I like the
work but it is tiring and excludes all else. I study when
I have time, and occasionally I dream. I play chess with
no serious opponents and I walk a great deal. I am losing
weight, partly from longing, and partly from the work.*

*Give a kiss to the little pieces of my flesh and blood and to
the others. For you, a kiss filled with sighs and sorrow from
your poor, bald*

Husband

In general, that was the tone of his correspondence, which was
infrequent and offering few details, although he was usually
optimistic about the prospects of the ELN (the National Liberation
Army of Bolivia). In a way he was right to be optimistic; I later
heard about the courageous actions they had carried out as a small
group of combatants facing a better-equipped army with more
men. It was this optimism that never allowed me to contemplate
the final outcome.

Meanwhile, my life carried on as usual; the security garrison was now smaller, but was still next door to our house.

Occasionally, Fidel would become worried about us and pay us a visit, always mindful of our needs. In fact, when Che wrote his "Message to the Tricontinental," Fidel brought the document to my house to tell me what he thought of it. This was not really necessary, but that is how Fidel was with everything concerning Che. He never failed to update me on the progress of the guerrilla movement in Bolivia.

My commitments had changed somewhat. Before leaving for Bolivia, Che urged me to enroll at the university to study history, which I did in November 1966, and I must admit that he was not wrong. This proved to be a wise decision because I now used part of my time to study, clinging to it almost as a shipwrecked sailor clutches at his salvation.

I made a big effort, and took advantage of the opportunity I was presented with. I was studying with younger people, with the exception of María Luisa Rodríguez, who was older than me, and she became my study partner. She was very organized and capable; she was also the head of her household and didn't want to stay at home. Despite her wealthy background and her privileged life, she responded like all Cuban women did to the demands of the times.

I studied with enthusiasm and tried to adapt myself to a study routine. Compared to the other students, I had far more life experience, but it was difficult for me to concentrate on my studies. My classmates and teachers helped me, showing me great kindness in a situation new to me. I was grateful to Che for encouraging me to step into a very different world and out of the isolation of my own little world.

∞

The month of October came around again. I heard the terrible news from Fidel. He waited until the report from Bolivia had been verified. At the time, I was involved in some important research work in the Escambray Mountains as a history student.

Celia Sánchez traveled to Santa Clara, and from the airport she organized for me to be picked up and taken directly to Havana, where Fidel was waiting for me. He took me to his house, where I stayed on my own for one week. I then went to stay in another house for a while with my children. Fidel visited us every day. I can never forget the kindness and dedication he showed us during those days. He gave us so much of his time and helped to ease our pain. Appreciating his tenderness, I was aware that he, too, was deeply mourning the irreparable loss that Che's passing represented.

Since that time, in spite of the fact I don't see Fidel regularly because of the immense responsibilities he has borne, nothing has ever marred our mutual affection and the solid basis of our friendship. Everyone acknowledges the debt we Cubans owe him, but my debt is far greater on a personal level.

On October 18, 1967, a solemn vigil for Che was held in Revolution Plaza. Fidel was the only speaker. He asked me to be there, but I told him I didn't have the strength to behave with the composure demanded of me in such a ceremony. I told him I would stay at home, watching the event on television, surrounded by my children, although they were not yet aware of what had happened.

The vigil in the plaza was a moving event for our people. I had never seen so much sadness reflected in the faces of the men and women, who came to the plaza in absolute silence to pay homage to the legendary guerrilla, the brother they had always felt was one of their own.

I returned to my own home in November, accompanied by my offspring, who were noisy and restless and allowed me little time to become absorbed in my grief. I had to get on with life, I had things to do. But there were the inevitable moments when I would hear the verses of the poem he had written for me:

My only one in the world:
I secretly extracted from Hickmet's poems this sole romantic
verse, to leave you with the exact dimension of my affection.

Nevertheless,
in the deepest labyrinth of the taciturn shell,
the poles of my spirit are united and repelled:
You and EVERYONE.

Everyone demands complete devotion from me
so that my lonely shadow fades on the road.

But, without ridiculing the rules of sublime love,
I hide you in my saddlebags.

(I carry you in my insatiable saddlebags, like our daily
bread.)

I leave to build the springs of blood and mortar
and I leave in the vacuum of my absence
this kiss with no fixed address.
But the reserved seat was not assured
in the triumphant march of victory,
and the path that guides my travels
is overcast by ominous shadows.

If my destiny is an obscure seat of honor in the foundations,
just place it in the hazy archive of your memory,
to use during nights of tears and dreams...

Farewell, my only one,
do not tremble before the hungry wolves
nor in the cold steppes of absence;
I take you with me in my heart
and we will continue together until the road vanishes...

9

After I returned home, my life continued, despite incredible difficulties. The images from that time are confused in my mind. The sad reality was that I felt the absence of the man who had been my first love and the one with whom I had shared the best and fullest moments of my life. I thought it would be impossible to overcome so much pain. But I was not alone, and I heard his voice ringing in my head: "Help me now Aleida, be strong..."

Somehow I kept on with living and focused on the large and small details that surrounded me and which slowly filled my existence. I gave myself to my children with an overwhelming need to find refuge in their company.

We were a single unit: I was then 33 years old and my children were seven, five, four and two years old. The older ones had started school and the younger ones were in childcare. The mornings began with tears, hurried breakfasts and dropping off the children at their respective places, before I went off to study. This meant that in the midst of the domestic chaos engulfing me, I traveled a road that was not lonely. I had a boisterous home that I did my best to maintain so the children could get through that difficult period less damaged. As César Vallejo says, I lived, "with no news and no green pastures," "only two old roads that are curved and white/That is where my heart travels." But time passed.

In 1968 I was in Trinidad, a city in the former province of Las Villas, where I was doing work related to my studies when Fidel unexpectedly sent a message asking to see me. This took me by surprise because I had never imagined that I would have the diary Che had written in Bolivia in my hands in such a short space of time. It had been sent to Cuba in extraordinary circumstances, thanks to the audacity, courage and solidarity of some of our friends.

I was asked to collaborate in the deciphering of Che's handwriting, which was very difficult to do. I agreed to take on the task, and began working on it with complete dedication, along with Vidalina, Manuel Piñeiro's secretary. We worked in absolute secrecy. Once again I was touched by Fidel's delicate gesture toward me. While it was true that Che's handwriting was sometimes illegible, there were other people who could decipher it without my help. I have always asked myself if Fidel really needed my assistance or if he felt the need for me to be one of the first to read that extraordinary document.

The publication of the diary had a big impact and raised many questions only the passage of time has been able to answer. The entire world was shaken by what was contained in those pages, and Che's *Bolivian Diary* became one of the most important documents in the history of our continent, revealing not just the universal impact of its protagonists but of the immense figure of Che himself.

Cuba had the privilege of publishing Che's diary for the first time in a massive print run that was distributed free in June 1968, less than a year after his assassination. The book was in every Cuban bookstore where there were long lines of people waiting to read it. This was unprecedented in the history of Cuban publishing. We Cubans felt Che was with us again, and we were inspired once more by his incredible courage.

My feelings about this now, after so many years, are very hard to explain, because even though I worked on the transcription of Che's *Bolivian Diary*, I have never been able to read it again. I have looked at fragments, checked dates and details, but I have never been able to sit down and reread it. I feel too much pain at those final, lonely moments, when I was not there with him to comfort him. I not only remember the brave man and resolute guerrilla fighter that I always knew. I also think about other aspects of that remarkable human being of so many different dimensions, a man who gave himself completely to his love for humanity, a man who was finally assassinated in a brutal way, without his executioners ever considering the magnitude of what they were doing.

CB

Our children grew up and I finished my university studies, while continuing to play a role in the FMC. After I had graduated, I worked with the Ministry of Education in the preparation of school texts about the history of Latin America, along with a group of researchers from the institute. One of my projects was to put together a historical atlas of Latin America. In that way, I immersed myself in the study of the region, and for some years, up to the 1980s, I worked at the Center for Studies of the Americas (CEA). I focused particularly on Argentina and the labor movement in that country. Obviously, I felt a strong tie to Che's homeland.

In 1975 I was nominated and later elected as a deputy to the National Assembly of People's Power. I became the first president of the commission for foreign relations and in that position I had great pleasure in working with Raúl Roa, a close friend of Che's who, at the time, was vice-president of the National Assembly. He was an extraordinary man, very cultured, tender, loyal and totally committed to the revolution. He had a wonderful, incisive sense of humor that was very Cuban.

During this period, I had the privilege of accompanying Roa on various international tours. He gave brilliant speeches in defense of Cuba's interests and policies and international political issues that reminded me very much of Che's approach and style. Everyone who had the opportunity to work with Roa learned a great deal, and we could see the respect he inspired from both friends and enemies. He became known in Cuba as the "Foreign Minister of Dignity."

I took on other responsibilities in the National Assembly until my term as deputy ended in 1991.

Meanwhile the children became adults and chose their different pathways. I tried to guide them as best I could so they would not feel the absence of their father too badly or feel too burdened by expectations. I kept in mind Che's comments in his story, "The Stone":

> Our children? I would not want to live through my children. They don't even know me. I am just a foreign body that occasionally disturbs their peaceful existence, getting between them and their mother.

> I imagine my oldest child, and she, now with gray showing in her hair, is saying, "Your father wouldn't have done this, or that..." Inside myself, the child of my father, I feel a tremendous sense of rebellion. As a son, I would not know whether or not it was true that, as a father, I would not have done such-and-such a thing, or had done something badly. But I, as my son, would feel vexed and betrayed by this memory of I, the father, being rubbed in my face all

the time. My son had to become a man, nothing more, not better or worse, just a man. I was grateful to my father for his sweet and un-selfrighteous displays of affection.*

I think of our four children as men and women, nothing more. The oldest, Aleidita, is a pediatrician; the boys, Camilo and Ernesto, are lawyers; and Celia is a veterinarian, specializing in dolphins and seals.

Over the years, I have tried to resist becoming petrified as a statue of the grieving widow. I eventually remarried. Somehow I have found the strength to go on living.

I have been acutely aware of the need to keep Che's real legacy alive and I discussed this with Fidel. He asked me whether I would consider turning our home into a museum. After reflecting on this, I thought that instead of a museum the house should become a center focusing on the study of Che's life and legacy. Fidel sent me a message, agreeing to the proposal, suggesting we begin working on it as soon as possible.

I knew the responsibility this entailed. It also meant I would have to move to another house, leaving behind, as Martí put it, the "yoke and star" I had borne for many years. As I packed up my memories again, in preparation for moving house, I was content knowing that the new project would complete something Che had left unfinished.

I was convinced the best thing we as Che's family could offer the Cuban people and others around the world who admired him was to properly organize his personal archive, his unpublished papers, documents, photos and all the commentaries about him. The Che Guevara Studies Center has since become a place of study and reflection, presenting the enormous body of his creative thought and the example of his life and work.

---

* Che's short story, "The Stone," is included as an appendix to this book.

What better way to get to know Che than to discover him by looking through the book and photo collection that formed his library? You can see how he tried to improve himself as a human being in his writings on culture, philosophy, history, and medicine, and the way in which he approached social projections and clinical investigations on allergies.

The Center's role in showcasing studies and research on Che's life and work is something I dreamed about for decades. The Center is also collaborating with Ocean Press and its sister Spanish-language project Ocean Sur in the publication of Che's complete works, including thematic collections of his writings as well as his famous diaries, from his travels in Latin America as a medical student on a motorcycle through to his last *Bolivian Diary*.

One of the Center's priorities has been our community work and cultural activities within the community. These include workshops in computer skills, ceramics, film screenings, lectures, participation in national events and photographic exhibitions.

As part of our goal to demonstrate various aspects of Che's life, the Center currently has a traveling exhibition called, "Che the photographer." This has been greatly admired by those who have seen it, discovering an unknown aspect of Che's talent, especially his aesthetic sense and technical skill. Che enjoyed photography from the time he was an adolescent, and throughout his life his camera became an essential accomplice by his side. In Cuba, and on his many trips through Latin America and the world, he took hundreds of photographs of whatever captured his attention.

These few examples of our work today help show how Che's story and his example have struck a chord among many people throughout the world in a way he could never have imagined.

During these years, which have been both long and short at the same time, the story and figure of Che Guevara have grown to occupy a prominence worldwide, never before imagined. Finally, I can affirm as his most faithful and loyal admirer that I saw how Che made himself, how he grew spiritually, through his dedication to the just cause of creating a better world.

10

One day toward the end of 1995, I received the call I had both hoped for and dreaded. I was told that—almost 30 years after his assassination and secret burial—Che's remains finally might have been located in Bolivia.

Of course, I had known that one day this might happen. Nevertheless, I was in complete shock, my feelings quite contradictory. Like Che, I believed a combatant's body should remain in the country where he or she had died if they were killed on an internationalist mission.

Che was right about that, but I asked myself if that is what I really wanted. Had I accepted this argument as a defense mechanism to avoid facing something so very painful? In the end, however, the decision wasn't mine. As soon as our people learned of the possibility of finding Che's remains, and those of the other compañeros who died in Bolivia, they wanted the search to begin.

It took almost two years of arduous work to find what the Bolivian military had jealously guarded as their "war trophy." But the dignity of the Bolivian and Cuban peoples was eventually recovered along with that of those "with stars on their foreheads."

One cold morning on June 28, 1997, the remains of seven fallen compañeros were exhumed from an unmarked grave at Vallegrande, Bolivia. The news of Che's death had shaken the world in 1967. Now the discovery of the grave that had held his remains for more than 30 years, reignited international interest in his life and legacy. At a time when the world was undergoing many difficult trials, such as the fall of the socialist camp in Europe and with hegemonic neoliberalism reaching into every corner of the globe, it was as though Che had risen again, challenging us to take on new battles. After a thorough process of identification, the remains arrived in Cuba on July 12, 1997, and were received by the heroes' families and compañeros. My children helped me to have the strength to face the small ossuary that had come from far-off Bolivia. Che had now come to his final resting place in the country he had adopted as his own. At the welcoming ceremony, with a mixture of pride and infinite pain, I heard the voice of my daughter Aliucha speak in the name of the families of the fallen. She put into words what we all felt. Addressing Fidel and all those present, she said:

Dear Commander,

More than 30 years ago our fathers said good-bye to us. They set off to continue the ideas of [Simón] Bolívar and [José] Martí in a continent united and independent. But they never lived to see a triumph.

They were aware that these dreams can only be achieved through immense sacrifice. We children never saw our fathers again. At the time, most of us were quite young. Now as grown men and women we are experiencing, perhaps for the first time, the pain and intense sadness of our loss. We know what happened, how our fathers died, and we suffer as a result.

Today their remains have been returned to us, but they do not return defeated. They return as heroes, eternally young, courageous, strong and daring.

Nobody can take that away from us. They live on, united with their children and their people.

They knew that they would return one day, that our people would welcome them with love and would heal their wounds. They knew that you, Fidel, would continue to be their friend and leader.

That is why we ask you, Commander, to honor us by receiving their remains, the remains of those who are more than just our fathers; they are the children of this land that you so honorably represent. Receive your soldiers, your compañeros, who have returned to their homeland.

We also give you our lives.

Hasta la victoria siempre! [Until victory, always!]

Patria o muerte! [Homeland or death!]

These words, spoken by the eldest of my children, contained the respect and admiration that only a people like the Cubans know how to express. In Havana's Revolution Plaza, under the gaze of the gigantic statue of José Martí, where three decades earlier Che's death had been mourned in utter silence, now a sea of people in a never-ending line welcomed back their legendary hero.

The same thing happened in every province the funeral procession traveled through until it finally arrived in Santa Clara, the scene of Che's most famous battle, where a plaza had been built in his memory.

This time I was not returning to my hometown to meet old friends and remember happy times. I went to say good-bye and to perform a little ritual I felt I owed him. No one else, not even my children, knew what I had decided to do. I had given Che a small black scarf as a keepsake when he left for the Congo. When we met up again in Tanzania, he returned it to me. He mentions this scarf in the short story, "The Stone." Writing in a sorrowful mood after learning his mother was dying, he ponders his own mortality. Despite his characteristic ironic tone, it is clear how much he cherished that modest scarf:

> Ah, the gauze scarf—that was different. She gave it to me in case I injured my arm, in which case it would make an amorous sling. The problem was if I were to crack open my nut. But then there would be a simple solution: it could be wound around my head to tie up my jaw and then I would take it with me to the tomb. Loyal even unto death.*

So late one night, when everyone had left and I was alone with my daughters staring at the small coffin, I asked Aliucha if we could open it. There was something I had to do, I explained. In the end, I could not find the strength to do what I wanted to. So it was my daughter Celia who placed the scarf in the coffin with him, "Loyal even unto death."

The final ceremony took place in Santa Clara on October 17, 1997. Again, Fidel with incredible strength and composure under the circumstances found the precise words to capture the spirit of that moment. I knew better than anyone the enormous effort this cost him to express his ideas to our people.

Welcome, heroic compañeros of the reinforcement.

The trenches of ideas and justice you defended, along with our people, will never be conquered by the enemy.

Together we will continue fighting for a better world.

Hasta la victoria siempre! [Until victory, always!]**

---

* Che's short story, "The Stone," is included as an appendix to this book.

** See Fidel Castro: *Che: A Memoir* (Ocean Press, 2006).

So that is how our story ends. But the story continues with our four children, the little *trocitos** that we made together, and 10 grandchildren, who I hope will all love and appreciate their grandfather as he really was. My children have followed in their father's footsteps, volunteering for internationalist assignments in Angola and Nicaragua in the same spirit of solidarity and commitment to the just causes for which their father fought.

I think I can feel satisfied with my life and, when my time is up, I will say as Che did, "Think of me once in a while..."**

---

* Literally, little pieces.

** This is how Che signed off a letter to his parents when he left Cuba in 1965 to lead the internationalist mission in the Congo, Africa. See Ernesto Che Guevara, *Che Guevara Reader* (Seven Stories Press, 2022).

AFTERWORD

For someone who is not a writer by profession, it is very difficult to correct errors or omissions, which unfortunately remain when one has finished writing a book, especially if you are trying to unravel events from your memory and those events have assumed such historical importance.

On rereading my book, I feel that I have not sufficiently acknowledged many compañeras, women who played a key role in our struggle, with valor, selflessness and devotion. From my personal experience, there were many men and women from my province who acted with extraordinary courage, and I believe they should not be forgotten.

I want to at least mention them in this tribute, paying them the homage they deserve: Margot Machado, Ernestina Mazón, Dolores Rosell Anido, Digna Sires, Carmen Zapateros, Verena Pino, Marta Lugioyo, Teresita Orizondo, Zoraida Lugo, Nena and Clara Gómez Lubián, Luisa Díaz (the mother of Haydee Leal) and Melitina Delgado.

Haydee Leal's home was one of the places where our compañeros met, including the meetings of the first provincial leadership of the July 26 Movement, and where on various occasions they found refuge. Haydee's mother, Luisa Díaz, knew the risks she was taking, but she never hesitated and always welcomed us with a warm smile. Time has not erased that smile from my memory.

Another of those selfless mothers with extraordinary strength was Melitina Delgado, Marta Lugioyo's mother. Marta was a well-respected lawyer, who undertook numerous dangerous assignments for the underground revolutionary movement. She owned a car at a time when not many people had cars, and it was easy for her to move around in relative safety. When we used her mother Melitina's home, we never felt we were imposing on her. She knew the purpose of our meetings, and sometimes she had some compañeros to stay with her for short periods of time. We were always careful not to compromise this safe house, the home of Melitina and "Papito," as we called Marta's father.

In acknowledging these compañeras, I have by no means mentioned all those who contributed to the emancipation of our country and restored its dignity.

Appendix

THE STONE

Ernesto Che Guevara

This is one of several short stories Che Guevara wrote for Aleida during 1965 while he was in the Congo, Africa. While mourning the loss of his mother, he imagines the circumstances of his own death.*

He gave me the news in the way such things should be told to a tough guy, a man in charge, and I was grateful for this. He didn't hide his concern or his distress, and I tried not to show mine. It was as simple as that!

Besides, I had to wait for confirmation before I could mourn properly. I wondered if it was okay to cry a little. No, no, it was not possible. The leader cannot have personal feelings. It's not that he's denied the right to have personal feelings, he simply must not show them like his soldiers might.

---

* See Ernesto Che Guevara: *Congo Diary: Episodes of the Revolutionary War in the Congo* (Seven Stories Press, 2021) for his fascinating account of Cuba's assistance to the liberation movement in the Congo.

"It was a friend of the family who called to say she was seriously ill, but I wasn't there that day."

"It's serious—you mean she's dying?"

"Yes."

"Be sure to tell me if you hear anything else."

"As soon as I hear anything... But I don't think there's any hope."

Death's messenger left but I had no confirmation. The only thing I could do was to wait. When the news became official, I would decide whether or not I had the right to show my grief. I was inclined to think not.

The morning sun struck hard against the rain. There was nothing strange in this; it rained every day and then the sun would come out, making itself felt and removing the dampness. In the afternoon, the stream would be crystalline once again, although not much rain had fallen in the mountains that day. This was pretty normal.

"They said it stopped raining on May 20 and wouldn't rain again until October."

"That's what they said... but they say so many things that aren't true."

Would nature adhere to the calendar? I didn't care whether it did or not. In general, I didn't care much about anything at all—this forced idleness, this stupid war without a purpose. Well, maybe the war had a purpose, but it was all so vague, so diluted. Whatever its aims were, they seemed unattainable, like some surrealist inferno where tedium is the eternal punishment. It mattered to me. Of course it mattered.

I have to find a way of breaking out of this, I thought to myself. It was easy to work things out in one's head. You could make a thousand plans, each as tempting as the next, put two or three of the best together, simplify them, put them down on paper and deliver it. That was the end of it and then one started anew. Theirs was an unusually clever form of bureaucracy: instead of filing anything, they made it disappear. My men said they smoked it— any bit of paper can be smoked if there's something inside it.

There was an advantage to my mental pondering. What I didn't like could be changed in the next plan. Nobody would notice. It seemed like this could go on for eternity.

I felt like a smoke and took out my pipe, which, as usual, was in my pocket. Unlike my soldiers, I never lost my pipe. It was very important to me. One can travel any distance along paths of smoke—I would say plans can be created and victory imagined without it seeming like a dream, but more like reality made vaporous with the distance and the mist that is always present in smoke trails. It's a good companion, the pipe. How could they lose something so essential? What brutes!

They were not really brutes. They had done their work and were exhausted. So they didn't have to think, and what use is a pipe if not for thinking? One can dream. Yes, one can dream. The pipe is important when one dreams from afar, dreaming toward a future whose only path is smoke, or dreaming back to a past so distant it is necessary to retrace one's steps. Urgent yearnings are felt elsewhere in the body. They have vigorous feet and keen eyes and don't need the aid of smoke. My soldiers lost their pipes because they were not essential to them: things that are important are not lost.

Do I have anything else like that? Ah, the gauze scarf—that was different. She gave it to me in case I injured my arm, in which case it would make an amorous sling. The problem was if I were to crack open my nut. But then there would be a simple solution: it could be wound around my head to tie up my jaw and I would take it with me to the tomb. Loyal even unto death. But if I was left lying on the mountainside, or if somebody else picked me up, there would be no gauze scarf. I would decompose on the grass or they might exhibit me; maybe I would even appear in *Life* magazine, my desperate death gaze fixed at a moment of extreme fear. Because everyone is afraid. Why deny it?

Through the smoke, I followed old trails and reached into the most intimate corner of my fears. These were always linked to death, that disturbing and inexplicable nothingness. Inexplicable, however much we Marxist-Leninists like to describe death, with conviction, as just nothingness. What is this nothingness? Nothing. The simplest and most convincing explanation possible. Nothing is nothing. Shut down your brain, dress it in black robes, with a sky of distant stars if you please; that is what nothingness is — nothing. The equivalent of infinity.

One survives in the species, in history, that mystified form of life, in actions, in memories. Have you never felt a shiver run down your spine when reading of Maceo's machete charges?* That is life after nothingness. And our children? I would not want to live through my children. They don't even know me. I am just a foreign body that occasionally disturbs their peaceful existence, getting between them and their mother.

I imagine my oldest child, and she, now with gray showing in her hair, is saying, "Your father wouldn't have done this, or that..." Inside myself, the child of my father, I feel a tremendous sense of rebellion. As a son, I would not know whether or not it was true that, as a father, I would not have done such-and-such a thing, or had done something badly. But I, as my son, would feel vexed and betrayed by this memory of I, the father, being rubbed in my

---

* Antonio Maceo was a Cuban independence fighter against the Spanish.

face all the time. My son had to become a man, nothing more, not better or worse, just a man. I was grateful to my father for his sweet and un-selfrighteous displays of affection. And my mother? Poor old dear. Officially, I did not yet have the right to mourn her and still had to wait for confirmation.

I was wandering like this along the trails of smoke when a soldier interrupted me, pleased to be useful.

"You haven't lost anything?"

"Nothing," I said, associating this particular nothing with the other of my reverie.

"Check."

I felt my pockets. Everything was in order. "Nothing."

"And this little stone? I saw it on your key ring."

"I'll be damned!"

I was hit by savage self-reproach. One loses nothing essential, nothing vital. Is one alive if things are no longer necessary? As a vegetable, yes, but as a moral being, no—at least I don't believe so.

I felt the chill of memory. I found myself, rigorous, meticulous, feeling my pockets while the water flowed past, opaque with the mountain soil, hiding its secret from me. The pipe—first of all, the pipe—it was there. The papers or the scarf would have floated. The vaporizer present; pens here; notebooks in their nylon covers, yes; the matchbox, also present. All in order. The chill melted.

I had brought only two small keepsakes with me into battle, the gauze scarf my wife had given me and the key ring with the little stone in it from my mother, an inexpensive, ordinary thing. The stone had come loose and I kept it in my pocket.

Did that stream flow with mercy or vengeance, or was it simply dispassionate, like the leader? Does one not cry because one must not, or because one cannot? Is there no right to forget, even in war? Is it necessary to disguise a lack of feeling as machismo?

I don't know. I really don't know. I know only that I feel a physical need for my mother to be here so that I can rest my head in her bony lap. I need to hear her call me her "dear old fella" with such tenderness, to feel her clumsy hand in my hair, caressing me in strokes, like a rag doll, the tenderness streaming from her eyes and voice, the broken channels no longer bearing it to the extremities. Her hands tremble and touch rather than caress, but the tenderness still flows from them. I feel so good, so small, so strong. There is no need to ask her for forgiveness. She understands everything. This is evident in her words "my dear old fella..."

"Do you find it pretty strong? It affects me, too. Yesterday I nearly fell over when I tried to stand up. They probably didn't dry it properly."

"Yeah, this tobacco is shit. I'm waiting on the order to see if they bring some cut tobacco that's half-way decent. One has a right to smoke, even just a quiet and pleasant-tasting pipe, don't you think...?"